~The World~

One poem 27 topics

Emmanuel Wallace

~THE WORLD~

So THIS is the world we live in.
The home, place, and den
Where we all live side by side together as **kin**.
At least that was how it was back then,
Or was it?
I don't know what to tell you
But this world,
The world we live in today
 is far from unified.
Kinship does not exist in our **realm**
And we've long since given **hatred** the helm.
And it's driving us to hell.
We've allowed evil to ring the bell
Of this world.
THIS world is struggling to survive, beaten by pride
Yet it can't fight for itself.
I'm sure you know this
But you're probably wondering why I'm immediately
bashing this world.
I would be wrong to say that there is no good here
But I am saying that positive improvement is where
we need to be steered.
It only happens by our **desire,**
The start of the wire.
Then we go on to **relationships,**
The flavor of the chip before and after the dip.
We have to check our ambition.
It's the key in the ignition.
Our **argument** would be a lovely topic.
It's the number one thing that's continually toxic.

What about our **attention,**
Seems like we're all caught up in **superstition**.
We live in a world of **misfits** where everyone wants
a taste of **acceptance,** but would rather change
who we are to be distanced.
What is the extent of our **fame**?
What is the extent of our **fortune**?
What is the extent of our **happiness**?
Our **sadness**?
Our **joy**?
Our **peace**?
What is the extent of our short, short **lives**?
What is the extent of the condition of our world?
Is this not our world?
Where we live,
Breathe,
Walk,
Talk,
Laugh,
Cry,
Dance,
Shout,
Pout?
We are in a **drought,** my friend.
Without a reasonable doubt, we are losing our
connection with each other.
Social media,
I don't know, you tell me, is it *social*?
Or is it just *media*?
What are we feeding ourselves that makes us so
divided?
This world's direction is fairly one-sided.

At least if we don't change.
We both know what this is, this is a call to action
And I'm relying on you and your reaction.
It's not for me but THIS world.
For our world, our home until we die.
Will you join me for this ride in understanding what
we can do to make sure it is not our hand that tears
us **apart**.
Until we depart it's about time we **start**.
Our lives are each their own unique piece of art.
It doesn't matter if you're smart,
You could be a Bart.
It doesn't matter, be whoever you are as we go
through our world,
                    THIS WORLD, together.

~THE WORLD'S KIN~

Oh, how easy is it tainted?
Is it by power?
Or is it by pain?
Or could one say they both have a hand to play?
It isn't easy and it isn't hard to understand
That the eternal wave of brotherhood and
sisterhood lost
Is a result of love's decay…
We have become slaves to jealousy and envy.
I can say this because before, the world was not
known for its scores and stripes
But now it is wounded every which way from the
inside,
Where *we* ultimately reside.
The world's kin is us and them.

Us being the people
Them being the animals, plants, and environment
around us.
We are meant to coexist.
It's not something we should dismiss.
The bible says in Galatians 5:14 "...love thy
neighbor as thyself."
Is that so hard? Or do we prefer to bury each other
on dirty shelves?
We are made of the same substance
Yet we fight constantly to split ourselves apart.
Kinship is relation by blood
But I say it should be relation by love.
Kin in itself means family
But in our reality, we create castes that diverge us
From unity.
I will never say we will all agree on the same thing
But trust me, the more we fight,
the more the enemy wins.
Hatred is a work of the flesh and a key to sin,
And as kin, you can not tell me that that
atmosphere drags you in.
No, let me begin by saying, a divide in the house
will span forever as long as there is a north and a
south.
Not everything is right because someone decides
to rise.
Just because trouble is caused doesn't mean cave
in to that side.
I'm sorry but as your kin, I'm going to give you the
hard truth.

Just because we fight for, or over something
doesn't mean we're right.
We have these pointless arguments over what?
Instagram followers?
Now that's a sight.
We have to do better.
The platforms we create to connect
are driving us further and further apart.
There's no sign of an escape.
But it's not too late.
And because I love you,
I leave you with a choice
Will you choose peace and unity?
Or divide,
Allowing everything around us to decide how we'll
live our lives on the same earth
under the same pressure,
on the same rocky earth,
Tearing us apart on these weak grounds?
You decide your peace.
Freedom does not live in battles fought with guns,
Fire and brimstone,
Or disruptive homes.
We have to find it in our own
And make it known that sometimes a battle isn't
worth it.
Unify as one and we'd believe it.
If we'd take but one sip of love
There, we'll have kinship.
Sometimes the most influential battles are fought
through peace and unity.

The world around us should not be this far out of
sync.
Especially with all of this new technology.
We should protect the seas,
plant more trees, can't we see
Our air isn't getting cleaner
But neither is our deminer
we need to take control of our speedometer
And slow our fast selves down and
See what kind of influence we have on all that
suffers or grows around us.
It is our duty to uplift one another.
It is our duty to love like the one who died for us.
Whether you believe it or not
That is our last and final option for a cure.
A cure to the shade that makes us all obscure
Called hate.
We are kin to all we encounter.
we are involved in each other's lives, it is only right.
We must love even our enemies for we are not
judges.
And at the end of the day, he who uses the gavel
shall be judged the same if they are under the
same conviction.
If we live without trust and if we live without love
Nothing will ever change and at the end of the day,
we will keep falling.
So what's the point in stalling?
The choice is yours, mine,
Ours.
We are kin.

~THE WORLD REALMS~

It's crazy how we all live on one earth
But we are divided into a million different realms.
Realms are like alternate planes of existence,
the ultimate resistance
To conformity,
extending our personal livability.
We stretch it to the nth degree
And there are so many seeds
Like liberty (The desire to be free)
Nationality
Legality
And Reality.
These are just things that rhyme but trust me
It's by design
Because over time we've caused our own divide.
Why?
The World's realms vary
Our planes of existence vary.
Quite a few things were buried.
Battles between them have carried
The weight of this world to an imminent hole.
We pit the
Rich vs Poor
Wise vs foolish
Politic vs Politic
Religion vs Religion
Race vs Race
Star vs Star
Life vs Life
Fact vs opinion
Sex vs Sex

These are all realms we decide to live in
And it's by choice whether we believe it or not.
Each one is in a heated battle.
We are not aware that regardless of how beautiful
the escape we create, there will always be a tear.
Are we not aware that certain realms are right
And some are wrong?
Are we not aware that if we opened our ear
Maybe people wouldn't be trapped in fear?
This is why social media is the number one realm
Of today.
Because of this, our mental health has to pay.
This life is not a game where you can reboot.
Even in Minecraft, the game of realms
You have to scoot because
You're always fighting monsters.
The crazy thing is that the monsters that cause us
to hate and derate each other
Are buried on the inside.
The one realm we refuse to fight for is
The one we have to reside in
For our entire lives...
On the inside.
This is why we can't win
And this is why we won't ever win.
Because with all the made-up realms we
Create,
The one we refuse to regard until it's too late,
Is the one buried deep within our heart's gates.
How can this world thrive when nobody
understands the true problem?
Our focus.

We are focused on the right and left
When the answer is straight ahead.
Are our hearts dead?
Where are we blind?
Look at the times...
They're coming to a close
We'll be leaving this world row upon row.
And It will be a fatal blow,
Realms will rise and realms will fall
In the end, they all act as walls.
Especially when we pit them AGAINST
Each other.
We leave so many unnecessary stains and for
what?
Our pride?
It *must be*.
Our surroundings
Also known as nature
Is experiencing its own rapture.
It's by our hand's conviction
That hundreds of species are reaching extinction.
We might be next.
Life is a battle I guess,
Even those who wish for peace are at war.
Whose score are we trying to settle?
I hate to meddle but
do we win a medal
for our specified levels?
No.
We are fighting ourselves without even realizing it.
We choose realms that accommodate who we want
to be vs the person we are.

We do it in spite of something or someone.
Some of us choose them for the wrong reasons.
Do we just like fighting?
Do we think our hands are designed for smiting?
No.
A lot of us are fighting inside and it's spilling on the outside.
I am too.
I think sometimes battles are necessary,
But over every meniscal thing is a feat overdone.
Can we not listen to one another?
Its sickening how separated we are especially in the "land of the free"
We're far more trapped than we'd like to believe
And the media gives us the fuel we need
To head straight to destruction
It's like the only thing interesting to people is a good fight
It's all we see.
Prejudice
Superiority complexes
Truth be told both are vexes.
Let's move on to submission.
Some fights aren't worth losing and some aren't worth winning.
How can we save our realm, our home
THE WORLD...*EARTH*
Could we try not to suffocate each other?
This was the realm handed to us
And it is yet another one we neglect.
We'll be paying dividends.
Pick your battles wisely

Choose your crowd carefully
Choose where you'll focus whether it be
You or the world's view of who you should be.
The path to changing the world starts with us.
This world is judgemental,
This world is broken,
This world is void of essential elements,
This world is our home.
We can be the change the world needs
If we would fight and win the war within our internal
realm before going about slaughtering each other.
We all have but one set realm.
And that's our home, where we stand...EARTH.
We have always been a part of this realm.
Until we die, it's all we have
along with each other.
Understand that we are in this together.

~THE WORLD'S HATRED~

If I were the world I'd be fed up too.
I'd have to have my back polluted with people like
Me and you.
It isn't the world that hates though,
But it's inhabitants.
At our current rate,
the world will fight back.
Hasn't it already?
Sure it doesn't have guns and rockets
But it surely has a voice much more powerful.
You know, it's interesting how most of our battles
are fought for blood.
And at the end of it all, we resist the hugs,

The hugs of those who care about us.
We choose to hate an action or policy first,
Then we begin to project it toward a person or
group of persons.
Why does everything need to be projected as
such?
How much blood have we shed in an attempt to
pacify an idea?
We place the idea on a people and suit them as the
enemy,
And it occurs everywhere man exists.
It's like each sanction has its own hit list
And for what?
Power?
We need a shower.
Because this world reeks of hate.
Let me just say that our only escape
Free of this gate
Is what?
You already know what I'm going to say,
So where is it in this world?
Why is it buried so deep
when it's the essential quality we need?
It's crazy how it's something we flee.
We'd better roll up our sleeves because
Hate right now in *this world*
Has free reign.
And we have no one to blame but ourselves.
We have been blessed and cursed with the power
of choice.
It's strange how we can't listen to reason of voice.

I mean, of course, it's hard with all of the negative
noise and It becomes like an inescapable void...
A one-sided coin
I understand the talk of division, and hate is a hard
pill to swallow,
But still,
If we don't reveal the problems we have buried
within ourselves,
We'll end up stale and forgotten on the shelves.
Would you want to be that man or woman who is
remembered solely for how well they hated?
I don't think so
At least if you're not cynical
Hate is not clinical
It's mental.
Far below quintessential.
Change is essential
Unless we want to face the wrath of this world
before it's time.
Pop a bottle of wine and sit with yourself and ask
Who am I judging wrongly?
Whose life am I meddling with, with my opinion
unbacked by positive suggestions?
Why do I live to divulge my counterparts?
Why did I close this book?
Why do I gossip about pointless things?
Why am I afraid or reluctant to forgive?
Why am I reluctant to ask for forgiveness?
Who do I need to forgive?
Who am I?
What do I love or am I just so clouded with the
noise that It fades my true emotions?

I'll keep it simple,
LET IT GO
Where does hate get us when it acts like a
thousand-pound ball tied to our feet?
I am not asking for a utopia
where everything is perfect and at peace.
No
No
No
That would only be if everyone heeded the call of
love.
Factually that won't happen because as truth
stands there is a right and wrong in every situation
And some of us are entitled to this fact.
Life isn't always a competition yet we make it a
warzone.
You know love has a way of beating hate to a pulp.
I mean hate is going to be our downfall
So we might as well try love.
We could try talking instead of arguing.
We could try sitting instead of punching.
We could try serenity over shooting.
Peace over violence and ill tidings.
Now, hatred is an ongoing trend
One of the few ever to survive
More than a year
Just like fear
How does that appear in the eyes of those who
care about others?
Think of it as a scale
Hatred greatly outweighs love
Simple.

Factual.
Observable.
Unacceptable.
It is but a plague.
Love is the cure.
Life is the cure.
We will never live until we learn to let go.
Let go of the internal bounds that we project onto others.
Let go of the fear you're fighting to resist.
Let go of the disposition that you feel for being you.
Let go of the pain you experienced in the past...there is always a brighter future for those who believe.
Let go of perfection, there is no textbook in the world you could follow to reach that level.
Let go of the hate you have buried in your heart towards yourself.
Hatred begins with us and it spreads throughout the world because of such.
Even if it takes eons
Our kids
Our families
Our future
Needs light to lean on.
Trust me, hatred is not *that* light.
Our world is becoming the reflection of the darkness.
Is that how we want to live?
Because I know we don't have to live like this.
The world around us knows as well but it can't speak.

I can
We can.
I'm starting now by writing this book
You can start by sitting down and closing your eyes.
Breathe deeply and relax, loosen all muscles and
submit to the silence and utter these two words
"It's over."
They seem simple but if you submit to them you'd
know deep down that every dark thing placed in
this world can and will be replaced by the light.
I'm not here to tell you how your mind works
Just how love works.
The world we live in today can and will not stand
much longer unless we shift.
Competition is fun but war is not
Pain is not
Unnecessary suffering is not.
Malice is not.
We naturally will compete but greed can and should
not become our master.
It's funny how a piece of paper has rule over our
lives.
Dictates our ties and
Draws out or dark sides.
Its overarching value will become our demise.
If we let a dollar determine our level of
camaraderie, we'll be bound by envy our entire
lives.
Envy is but a root of hatred.
It's up to you to determine whether you'll water it or
strip it from your seed of greatness.
I won't tell you how to live but I will tell you this

There's a better path awaiting your arrival
But hatred is only going to drag you further and
further away from your destiny.
Remove hatred from the ignition
And replace the key.
You know what it is by now.

L

O

V

E

~THE WORLD'S DESIRE~

Ah, the fire of the world that makes it go round.
Like steam rises, we strive for natural things more
than anything.
We strive for fleeting things that last but a moment.
What do we desire that is fleeting?
Money
Fame
Fortune
Anything that makes us look good on most
occasions.
Items.
Why?
Because we live in a judgemental world where man
sets himself against man
And woman against woman.
We want what the next man has or the next woman
has.
What's the name of our culprit?
Envy, envy is its name.
It plays us like a game
Driving us insane

Chasing things that insert our hands for one
moment and into someone else's the next.
Desire is to strongly wish for or want something.
I won't say all of us are envious, no, some of us are
driven for success.
But at what cost?
What do we measure success off of?
I mean you can't possibly be successful without the
desire for more but
What is the extent of more?
I couldn't tell you.
I can tell you the brim of greed though.
It's almost like death row
A lot of us wish to decline its trough
But, inevitably, we can only slow it down.
The power of desire can easily be polluted with
greed by those who have shallow intentions.
What we desire as a material front will only drive us
to this conclusion.
Greed.
Simply put, greed is an intense or selfish form of
desire that ignites a fire that strives to eat up
Wealth
Power
Even food if it comes down to it.
The *world's* desire on the other hand,
Is mutual agreement and support.
But you know money, a brandished sheet of paper
that rules our lives is much more valuable, right?
I wouldn't say it's a bad thing but if that's going to
be
Our mission statement, just wait and see

How heavily this world will bleed
if we strive only for the green.
How can one lead when he/she is blinded
In a battle that is more or less one-sided.
If we'd widen
Our horizon
We'd be able to visualize
And realize
That there is more than what we can gain out there.
This world gives us
Food
Shelter
Nourishment
Comfort
Water
Air to breathe
Something beautiful to see
A reason to believe in something higher than me.
We should give also.
If a man were to snatch up all of the food in the
world
Would we deem him successful?
He achieved *his* goal.
But how do we feel?
The fact of the matter is that we only deem one
greedy when it puts us at a disadvantage.
Yes, it is a greedy act that sparks more greed.
His goal may have been achieved but for what?
Himself.
The problem is that greed is selfish.
The fact of desire is that it isn't overbearing

And it looks out for others in the process without force or disregard to the goal.
Competition is trumped when put against substance-based desire.
Anyone in search of substance will find it
Shallow desires will only drag you into the pit of greed.
The world's desire is simple.
The only way to true, fulfilling success is by serving and helping others.
Even if success can be reached on some level with shallow goals, eventually the further and further you go
The hungrier and hungrier you get and once you're starving it no longer matters who you have to trample to get what you want.
You would become a serial killer on the hunt.
So what kind of stunt
Am I trying to pull?
None at all.
It is what it is.
The world as it sits
Is full of selfish zits.
But at the brim of its lips
There's a drink it holds as a fix.
Purity is the main ingredient on the list.
It floats in the cup-like mist.
Just waiting for the refreshing touch of its kiss
Before digesting... it hits.
We need to have pure intentions when we choose what to desire or take action towards.
This world desires

Love
Joy
Peace
And a load of kindness.
Are we capable of giving it?
Of course.
It starts with us
Me and you
What we desire now, what is it?
Not only that but why?
Ask yourself this and you'll understand
What the world desires
Because when you add substance to what you
want
You'll understand what the true meaning of desire
is.
In a literal sense
Spiritual sense
And natural sense
Desire's true form is simple
It is the willingness to streamline our wants aside to
help others alongside us without growing envious of
what our counterparts possess.
what you have is nothing compared to what you
give.
What are you chasing that is more important than
what you see below?↓↓↓

~THE WORLD'S RELATIONSHIPS~

Camaraderie
mutual trust and friendship among people who
spend a lot of time together.
Friendship

a state of mutual trust and support between allied people.
Romance,
a feeling of excitement and mystery associated with love.
Acquaintance,
a person one knows slightly, but who is not a close friend.
Associate,
a partner, or colleague in business or at work.
Partner,
a person who takes part in an undertaking with another or others.
Relatives,
people connected by blood or marriage.
Teachers,
people who teach, especially in a school.
Student,
people who take an interest in a particular subject.
Winners,
people, or things that win something.
Losers,
a person or thing that loses or has lost something, especially a game or contest.
Givers,
people who give something.
Takers,
People who take something.
Our relationships are based on a whole list of titles.
Boyfriend
Girlfriend
Best friend

More friend
Less friend.
Guess friend.
There are so many forms of relationships that one
must incorporate their *own* blend
Of connection
Direction
and/or Complexion.
If I'm keeping it one hundred
It appears that
Of these essential life assets,
A few things drive them towards a casket.
Most of the time it can be summed up as
unnecessary racket.
Let's start with this,
Relationships are hard.
If you put any of your relationships into a pot
And let them boil for a second you will see
Just how quickly some bonds bleed.
Others may stick together and conjoin with the
seeds Of deeper integration between them and
you.
Not all relationships hold this to be true
Some never truly exist
It's like a name on a guest-only list
One can easily forge a signature
But one can not easily be erased because
it is often written in pen, on our hearts.
Like soup, one unintentional ingredient can shift the
whole dish
Which will make you wish that 11:11
Granted a wish that brought forth an alternate shift

In reality.
What are relationships?
Like I said earlier it can be defined by its many titles.
But each title has its definition just as
Each relationship has its formula for either success or failure.
Some hang on the brink of these extremes.
I call it the season of connecting,
The midway point.
A place of little significance
But of high density
A lot of us wish we could fade in and out of each other's lives
And I admittedly will agree that sometimes it's a necessary move in some cases.
No one or anything is perfect on this earth.
Doesn't it seem like sometimes we connect to disconnect later without the unction that
it's what that relationship supplies us that lasts longer than the actual relationship.
Pain is essential to growth if we'll let it teach us.
Most of us despise relationships because we've lost so many,
Most of us feel hurt because we see no signs of winning.
Worlds around us remain spinning,
Yet when one branch splits from our tree of friends
Our world stops.
It stops like it's been sitting on a rickety clock.
Tick tock
And all of a sudden boom!

Our bond is thrust into a tomb
Like babies fresh out of the womb
We have no idea what to do.
A lot of romantic relationships aren't even romantic
They're more or less anticlimactic
Stuck in eternal static
Because the connection is like a string
Easily cut by a simple edge
Same thing with friendships because
For some reason, substance is tossed in a shed.
You see, substance is the essential spice to all
great cuisines.
It mingles with the steam
It enhances with the heat
Tenderizes the meat
of the relationship where it was once weak
And takes one for the team.
When other factors become but a dream
Substance is what we need in any and
Everything.
We need a reason beyond ourselves.
Can you not hear the bells?
Since we're defining everything,
Substance is the quality of being
Important
Valid
Or significant.
What were all of those titles on that list again?
Never mind they were relationship stands.
Each one sells its own content.
But it all depends on the viewpoint you approach
them in.

If you approach friendship as a simple bond meant
to be broken then it's meant to be broken
If you approach romance as a game to play until
you find the right one
A game it shall be.
And you're probably thinking well I don't approach it
as a game...
Why do you approach it then?
What do you want from it?
Answer that question and decipher what it means
to be in a romantic relationship then let me know.
If we approach our familial relationships as
something simple and forced.
Simple and forced it shall be.
Whatever you want something to be
It will more than likely turn out that way *in your
eyes*.
At the end of the day what you expect is what you'll
get with the exception of other factors.
It's not always us
But we will always play a factor
Whether it be big or small.
Our relationships
Are the bread and butter of our existence.
I would say I hate to sound like a broken clock
But I'm not
because without love to some extent we would
Not survive.
Plain and simple
I'm not saying everybody out here should be trying
to put a ring on everyone they cross but I mean
We need respect

Patience
Kindness
Gentleness
Commitment
Opportunity
We need to have forgiveness
Faith
And an open mind.
Truth be told a lot of us are too afraid to expand our horizons.
Now, if someone tries to get you to break your morals,
No
But if they want you to grow then yes consider it.
Relationships are all together complicated and simple in the same breath.
Truth be told this last line is going to be the most important line of this piece and the only one you need to remember.
The World's relationships = Love * substance/ you

~THE WORLD'S ARGUMENT~

It's Between me and you, it says
You live on me and I provide for you
But hey, you neglect me, that's cool.
It's cold out here, not going to lie.
The environment out here is crazy.
It's going up in flames but i'm freezing
How does that make sense?
Tell me something,
Why when I take a whiff of air is it bitter?
Why when I scan my surface do I see trash?

Why do I feel the rumblings of war on my face and
Amongst *you*?
Haha that's funny!
For what reason besides personal desire do you
fight?
If anyone should be mad it should be me.
If you have a rebuttal please let me know.
Because I'd love to know who else is making me
suffer.
I understand rapid advancement technologically
But where is it socially
That's where the problem is coming from.
I don't care if the author talked about it earlier but
My friend
How much more hate
Are you going to brand me with?
All I ask for is a shift.
I am your world but you have total control
over how I play my role according to your goals.
Would you hear me if I called?
Would you care at all?
I know you'd say you do but do you?
I know of a select few that go unheard of
But how about you?
You know pain doesn't always last for just a second
Sometimes it leaves an irremovable scar.
But you wouldn't know that unless you looked at
your charts.
Let me break it down from the start
We started as friends where I provided most of
what you desired
But bring it to now it's boiling down to the last wire.

Evolution is good but where has it dragged us?
You and me?
You see although we are both entirely
Different entities,
Human and realm we're together as one,
Almost.
I am not living but the things upon me are.
I am but a representation of where you live
I am the world,
The home
Atmosphere
The environment in which you live.
I am the place you choose to neglect because I'm
humbly at your disposal.
But there *has* to be a change because just as you
suffer by your own hand, so do I.
Your actions blend and mix into my reality
The world you live in today is dying
And if you think I'm lying
Look around you
Door after door is being screwed
Shut, sharp, and shrewd
What do you lose?
Time
Same here...
We're on the same clock yet you treat me like
Chicken stock.
This world
Me
Well for the most part.
You cannot hear me call but
My signs are obvious

You broadcast them and they disappear
You argue amongst yourselves
But you take no action
You move to make progress
But stop in the middle
Where are you as humans truly going with your
Advancements?
To me, it seems further and further apart.
Each step is split.
This is my argument as the world
I expect your answer to be something like this.
The world is our home
And we must take care of it
But what matters most is production
Growth
Money
And overall stability in a human sense.
Those things I agree do matter.
But how could you do such in a world that is
running low on its necessary products?
Humans can create their own supply but how long
will that last?
To argue is to
give reasons or cite evidence in support of an idea,
action, or theory, typically to persuade others to
share one's view.
Take care of what you have and don't take it for
granted because the illusion of more is placed in
front of you on a pue.
Let me say this
Our lives are timed, so wouldn't you wish to bring
the place in which you dwell closer to a paradise

Rather than a filthy pair of shoes with parasites.
The only way this will stop is if we stop.
The world does not stop rotating because we wish
it to.
Time doesn't stop because we wish it to.
Change doesn't come because we wish it to.
We spend our lives working through loopholes
That burrow deep into this world's core
Like worms to an apple the more.
You...me...we are the change we need to settle the
score
Between destruction
And construction.
Change
And the eternal wave
(eternal wave of decay.)
But as the world says there is something missing
Something missing within our forces.
Our hearts,
Our very existence as a whole.
In the end, we need a much greater goal than
ourselves
The world has pleaded its case
Now it's up to us to either embrace this argument
Or deny it and evade it, the choice is ours as
always.
It's a superpower that if used wisely,
could crack the very brim of hate.
Every argument
Every question
Every decision
Every meaningful second

Every instance whether clear or unclear
Boils down to choice
All things big or small
Matter
Don't reduce your desire for better to unbeaten
batter.
Don't be like frightened bugs and scatter.
Or like chipped glass and shatter.
The reason you're afraid when I speak is because
You fear the power in which you cannot control
But that's not my role.
Initially
I'm here to thrive with you in unity
Perfect sync,
But that idea has become nothing more than a
heresy
That's not something I dare to bring
To the light of the scene
But believe you me
Our separation is a part of a bigger scheme
From day one it's become a recurring theme
Do you think we can't bleed?
We do
Some just hide it internally
We are not here to sit around and fend for
ourselves
We were not created to be like products and tools
we oh so carelessly leave on shelves
Or wells that are only valued by those who realize
that there is SUBSTANCE in the work they put into
receiving that which they earned,
Together.

Regardless of the weather
Regardless of the lack of shelter
Regardless of the lives that tethered
Near-death to lend a hand.
They that dug the well, became one with the world
And acknowledged it as a creation just like us,
Put here for *us (people)* to support
And to supply us also.
We're here for each other
And there's a reason why this planet
This earth
This world
Is the only one habitable.
We could try Mars but we can't change its natural
structure.
Why are we not satisfied with our home?
It's like a parent purposely neglecting their child.
That's wild because we as humans we think that
The earth is here only to provide for us
Eventually the more and more we kill it
We're going to have to rebuild it.
Simple as that, we have to take care of where we
live, like we take care of our car
We have to clean it,
Fuel it
And genuinely be careful with it.
We know how fast things can flip on us,
It's almost like colliding with a speeding bus
We won't see it coming until the deed is done.
As the hurricanes
The blizzards
The earthquakes

The floods
The world beneath us is being cut
Into tiny pieces.
There isn't much we can do anymore
With climate change rising
And losing its popularity
With the abuse of land and constant mining
Who knows what's brewing.
I don't
I won't
There is a message the world wants to get out and
you just read it.
Look into yourself
As I will myself and pray we have time
God bless it.
There should be a whirlwind of questions.
I have them too
I guess we both have some things to do.
Let's not be responsible for dragging our world into
And eternal tomb
At least not earlier than soon.
This world has made its case.
We can either make ours
Or pursue more than our own interest
And reach out beyond ourselves.
5 groups won't save the world alone
1 person won't either
I can't do it by myself
It's all of us
This is thus
And therefore an absolute must
That we join together in love.

The world pleads for it.
Don't let it fade to dust.

~THE WORLD'S ATTENTION~

Focus and attention
Two reasons why most kids get sent to detention.
Because they don't have either.
Priority and necessity
Two reasons why things get done and why some
are pushed aside.
Need and want
Two reasons why we war and peace.
We are in the least focused on these things.
At least on moral schemes.
The world's focus is similar to none other than ours
It seeks to protect itself
It seeks to nourish itself
It seeks to supply us (others)
Where it can be forced or unbothered.
The world's focus is on itself and others.
Although it is not a conscious being
it is an entity that can give and take away,
That's the world we live in today
As people.
We are in the world for a reason
And we are stripped from it also under the same air.
We give when we feel ready
We take whenever we need
Our expectations are off compared to where we live
We expect to receive when we are in need,
But we forget that since we only give when we're
ready

That essential help flow won't be as steady.
What are we focused on?
Where our attention has gone is
To the material world
Easy grabs
And simple drags
Anything to flee from the rags,
When internally we've been wearing them all along.
We've been singing the poor man's song,
Chasing an imaginary throne
"I want to be on top of the world!!"
For what
With what
Why?
A lot of us these days don't stop and ask these
questions
Especially the question,
Why.
This is understandable
It's not biodegradable
It only has one syllable
But it holds the most weight of any question ever
asked.
It'll make one think on a much deeper level than
they initially intended for themselves.
We often look for the easiest,
Quickest way out of a serious conversation
Especially when that question is raised
Why?
Why can't we answer the one question that
Focuses our claims?

Why is it so hard to reconstruct the way we hold our
reigns?
Can't we see we're rolling down the wrong lane?
What are we looking for?
The top of the world is the top of the world for only
a second.
Technically speaking we've only been on this earth
In this world
Comparatively for three seconds
And what have we really accomplished
According to our attention,
Or better yet intention.
What is our current position?
Our world is dying
That's a topic that's fairly trying.
What are we looking at?
Most of us at least
Are focused on money over peace
"Success" over where we plant our feet.
Why?
Why do we count it productivity
When our advancement
Is inflamed then,
Our only goal is to win.
Let's begin
We already know the world's attention
But we think we know ours.
Maybe individually but how about extensively
Beyond ourselves.
How many welds between us,
Between us and our world
are strong?

if they're beaten
Over time they'll weaken.
Man we're tweaking
It's crazy how we talk about "get your money up"
But trees are being chopped down thinner and
thinner
Our focus is a must.
To be honest there isn't anything wrong
With being successful
But what are we missing in this pursuit?
I can't say I have all the answers because I'd be
lying.
But on who and what are we relying
On to make a difference?
Is that option not listed?
If so I might've missed it
Because the people looking
Like me can't find them
It's like a one in a million cent.
It's like for wholesomeness you have to pay rent
To be seen
Imagine if we could see what all of the dreamers
around us who wish for a brighter future and earth
could see.
but our eyes are too flooded with
Distractions and insubstantial girth.
What is it that contributes to our worth?
Our world's worth.
Likes?
Follows?
Shares?
Okay.

The problem with that is we focus more on the
distraction than the attractions to change.
Why do we focus so much on copying the next man
when the world needs new solutions?
I'd hate to draw conclusions
You can call them delusions
Listen closely though
This is the world's resolution,
There is room to grow
And this is definitely not a show
On the low
We have to retrain our focus
We have to show up.
Imagine if this world would just glow up
It's far too dark.
The world is looking for the spark
Take that to heart.
Because what are we looking for?
Eventually, my friend, numbers
On the scoreboard are just numbers
And they're wiped at the end of the day.
In our case, that day is our life.
We are granted access in this world
For only a moment.
If we think about it, we always say "live in the
moment"
Well, we've been living it our whole lives.
This moment is for what we're trying to accomplish
not just for ourselves, our counterparts, and
whatever else; But for our world as well.
It can be as simple as raising awareness and

Building a bond with a small group of
world-changing individuals who are looking for
more.
It could be planting a host of trees
Or simply picking up some trash.
This moment is simple yet we overcomplicate it
With ideologies fixated on selfish gain.
But do the clouds rain for themselves?
Does the sun shine for its own pleasure?
These things are inanimate
So of course the answer is no because they have
no direct desire.
They serve their purpose continuously without fail.
What makes us different is the fact that we have
the power of choice.
Whose purpose is it to serve?
Look around you
Look around this world
It's all we can do to stay humane.
This world provides for us without fail
Because its purpose is to serve.
That's its focus
And if only we'd see that the most successful
people are the ones who provide for others.
I'm certain you've heard this before but this goes
back to desire.
Although we know this,
What is fueling our fire?
Why are we doing what we choose to do?
What are we focused on?
Our impact,
Or our income?

Where is our focus?

It's as if over time we lose our desire to accomplish something bigger than just surviving and looking cool.

We say we seek freedom but at a price.

There's nothing wrong with individual success and wealth

Nooo not at all I encourage you to strive for such things.

My only request is to remember your starting goal.

Because if that were to get tainted,

What are you sacrificing to meet social standards?

Society has the power to mold us into carbon copies of each other with no real motive.

So a lot of us seek fame over substance

Money over value

Luxury over sustainability

With no clear motive but to be as the next "millionaire."

How often is it besides the big names do we see people on the move to change the world even before catastrophe strikes?

Why?

Well, is anyone focused on the issues before they start?

Nope.

We need to rearrange our priorities

I mean we have an issue already with minorities

Seniority, conformity, and so many more of these.

But truth be told this world isn't here to separate

Segregate

Delegate

Or even dedicate its resources to just one group.
It's here to serve, are we?
But we're so caught up in the ropes of quieting
dreams to conformity that we just can't see
That although there are things posted out there that
are inspiring,
Wiring and plain out motivating
They aren't seen.
What are we focused on?
And why?
Ask yourself this and maybe you'll be the one to
realize the key to subside our landslide to the dull
side of the inside.
The world's attention is on us while ours is what we
deem worthy of a subscription.
Where is your, our attention?

~THE WORLD'S SUPERSTITION~

I wouldn't necessarily call this a superstition.
But the world has a vision.
A direct premonition
On how to develop a mission.
To end the relational distance
Between comfort and change.
It says we must give up comfort and embrace
change
We would much rather prefer that statement
rearranged,
Because although one generates gain the other
Shields us from the rain of defeat.
We act as if the ground will crumble beneath our
feet

If we dare try to move away from the things that
have buried us like stones to a cave.
We think to remain still is to avoid all blame,
Evade the wave of shame.
We treat life as a game
We must win against each other when ultimately
our main boss is ourselves.
We say change is unnecessary because things are
great just the way they are.
We are comfortable in a dirty world
Trashed by our hand.
People are dying but since it's not us who are
crying,
It doesn't matter.
We can be as carefree as we want if nothing veers
off course.
The *ideal* course of complacent "peace in torment."
We are tormenting ourselves with our lack of action
This is the reason why massacres still happen
Why the unjustified murder of innocent people
happen,
Why children are being abused, families are being
torn apart,
Why this world is crumbling with hate and
cumbersome darkness.
Our hope in comfort in darkness has left us
heartless.
That's why this is the world's superstition,
a widely held but unjustified belief in supernatural
causation leading to certain consequences of an
action or event, or a practice based on such a
belief.

Comfortability in where we are as a society is the
reason why change in the world is a backboard
propriety.
We're digging our own grave.
Look at the hole that we've made
For our future generations to fill.
It's like writing a will and passing down nothing but
unpaid bills
expecting them to straight-up kill
The process of covering our spill
After we're gone.
Change and comfort work hand and hand
But our interpretation is far too bland
We choose one hand or the other
Forgetting that the right is like the left's brother
There's a string attached to them that we can't see
Change brings forth the idea of comfort
And comfort is the product of change
The true pain is the fact that we found comfort in
the insanity around us.
We're ok with it.
Take a birthday child with no wish
You wonder why that is.
Is it because he has what he needs?
Or is it because he just can't think because
everything around him has been the same his
entire life and there is no drive to extend outward.
This is why our world today is so dark
Because we are living in the past regardless of how
we advance.
Technology cannot end racism, sexism,
sexualization, massacres of hope.

Alone it can't, yet we hide behind it like it's a shield.
We are the ones with the power to *use* it to make a change,
But we rarely do.
Our ground is crumbling beneath our feet and it is only when we begin to fall that we begin to see.
We've been falling for a while.
Some of us have barely managed to grab a chute.
Even so, that doesn't save you in a bottomless pit of comfort in the darkness.
Have we forgotten the stars?
There are so many but we only pay attention to a few.
like when we look at the people who choose to fight for more.
It's a shame that so many great leaders for peace are dead today.
So many advocates for grace were laced with pain by the hands of their alleged human brethren.
Are we not human anymore?
Because if we stay the way we are as a whole, we'll end up no better than pampered moles.
Hiding from the realities of life through the "protection" of our comfort.
There are two forms of comfort as you may assume.
I am speaking on peace and tranquility, unity with all surroundings, a warm feeling of relaxation and embrace.
No.
I am talking about the refusal of change also known as stagnation and complacency. The

acceptance of where we are without the slightest inclination of just how far away we are from the car of opportunity for far, far more beyond.

How long will we accept these social divides?

Is it our pride or our lack of it holding us back?

Who has the power here?

I know for a fact that superiority is a complex built like a curse,

It only exists because the blood we spill is quenching its thirst.

But first

Answer me this,

Why?

Some might say "people are gonna do what people are gonna do so why not?"

People die because of it.

It's tragic how the loss of life on this planet *especially* unjustly doesn't matter to us unless we are a part of the victimized group.

It's tragic how tragedy sparks action but we wouldn't notice otherwise.

How many people must die before they are broadcast?

How much pain is inflicted amongst others that we don't see?

We can't use everything as an excuse to hate one another.

We would rather embrace one another to change something permanently.

Everything in life is temporary except the lessons passed down from generation to generation.

If you show them it's okay to sit back and watch
hate prevail, what do you think they'll do until it
comes knocking at their door?
The distance is between us.
The relational difference between change and
comfort, is us.
Too many of us are comfortable ignoring reality.
our new life in totality.
Is this a superstition or a dilemma?
We're tied in a knot of confusion.
A rope twirled expertly by illusion.
While we thrive in our complacency
Others die for their race it seems.
Everyone's light is not green...
But without a change, we would not see
That the danger lights are flashing
And flashing.
Yet we are not dashing
 to fix them.
But at home, we'll hum a conservative hymn.
Things have to change for us to grow
And to be able to take care of each other.
Sure some things are wrong but
 It is a must that we find a solution without death.
Not everything needs to change,
Our mode of action needs to be rearranged.
None of us want to accept the blame
But we are just as guilty as the next man who
initiated the claim.
When will we step up and realize that
Our world is hanging on its last lines
Yet we're trapped in ourselves

By our own vines.
We all need help
Me included
Love cannot be substituted by material things
We can make claims on how money can buy you
happiness and how it can't.
But we can also make claims on how without love
we will drown in the blood of our own being.
The love of money is the root of all evil
But loving each other is the staple of growth.
For those who claim religion and step away when
someone comes from the outside for help, are you
no better than he?
For those of us who claim we are superior but need
to kill and harm to prove it, are we no better than
the man that is dead?
For those of us who claim that what is wrong is
right because you say so, does that not mean the
man or woman opposing you is right also?
For those of us seeking things in vain to feel like
we're making a change when instead we keep
sinking, are we no better than the titanic?
For those of us who believe that two of the same
poles of a magnet connect and are switchable
however you please when we know factually that
neither principle works; Are you no better than a
rock in the sea?
What cause are we fighting for that has nothing to
do with making our world better?
There are a lot.

I could name a few but I will say that the conservatives of today and yesterday are not wrong in their downward opinion on a few.
How much better am I, the author of this book, than the man or woman reading this exact page? Not at all.
We are seen in the same light which means in the end we'll be judged the same also.
My God is fair in his way
So let me just say,
that you must be saved from this hate....
Because the truth of the matter is that a lot of us are afraid.
We don't know what will happen if we pursue something uncertain.
The answer is to roll away the curtains covering your heart.
Have we forgotten that they beat for a reason?
Maybe we have.
God has allowed it to become a symbol yet I find it hard to find anyone who resembles such beauty.
Jesus died for us so we may be free from the bond of sin, confusion, and comfort in the darkness.
I say these things truthfully,
A world without a heart cannot live,
Just as a man without a heart cannot truly be satisfied with who he is.
Is freedom not what we seek?
It doesn't matter the brand of society,
Is. This. Not. What. We seek?
Right now we reek of hate, envy, depression, and anxiety.

These are formed by the lack of love.
The problem is that these things have more power
because there are more of us drinking from their
cup.
There is a small minority of the 7 billion people in
popularity who choose the opposite.
It's like Acts 2:38
This is more than just a measly verse of the bible
because It calls for revival.
A new birth if you will.
The key to where freedom is instilled.
An escape from the poison darkness has spilled.
Repentance is the turning away from darkness
Baptism in the name of Jesus Christ(one name
alone) is the washing away of starkness
And to be filled is to be reborn in a new light.
This is the key to the freedom we seek but it
doesn't come as easily as 1,2,3
There is more to the equation
It requires faith and determination
To make the delegation
To change completely and entirely for better.
In order for us to be free, we must free ourselves
from the sinful (dark) bonds we wear.
If you aren't serious then you wouldn't know
That the golden rule is as so,
Love thy neighbor as thyself but I mean if we don't
want that then the opposite is what we'll get.
I can't say that everyone is this way.
It's one of few ways that we embrace positive
change.
Change over comfort

Comfort for change
Blame no one for it starts from within.
Every one of us has a part to play.
Light is slain by the darkness of today.
It's become the ultimate price paid for comfort
without change.
Why is it that goodness fades?
Hope is in the shades
Love is planted in the gray
Is the world's superstition inadequate?
I'll let you decide.

~THE WORLD'S MISFITS~

The number of us that hide ourselves is immense.
What are we hiding from?
Would the people of this society accept you either
way?
I mean if you hide you'll never know.
If you turn around blind when you're needed,
Your whole purpose could be defeated.
Why let darkness slide when you were born to be a
light?
Is it because "it's safer if you remain out of sight"
Because you're a misfit?
If you don't fit the criteria of society.
Which in today's time is to be a replica of the
person beside you.
Either you do what they do or you do nothing at all,
It sucks because if you try something new you're
practically screwed with the wave after wave of
copycat stew.

A misfit is someone who characteristically doesn't
fit the majority,
It's almost like being a minority
Because we are few and easily categorized
And with our significance unrealized
We will subside into dust.
Why do we feel urged to lust
After acceptance?
Where am I going with this lesson?
Who are you?
Ask yourself this
And who you are won't be missed because
This is not a question like
What's your name,
How old are you,
Or even what do you like?
It is simply asking, Who. Are. You?
It's so simple it's hard.
What are we looking for in ourselves that we think
we can find in everyone else?
Look in the mirror and understand we are all misfits
in our own right.
Everyone says we're different but they never
express it.
Rarely accept it.
A single trait does not define you,
Your humanity does.
If you were all alone on this earth how would you
feel?
Lonely?
Distraught?
Uncertain?

Comfortable maybe?
Free?
How soon would it be until you lose hope?
Look in the mirror again and see how you feel.
At the end of the day
You are the one you have to live with.
If you let the pressure of the world outside reform
you into a lesser version of yourself
What are you losing?
You are realistically losing a portion of yourself.
Who do you make yourself out to be?
Just another person with a meaningless existence?
Nah see that's the problem,
As I mentioned earlier, there is little desire to
change in this world.
Instead, we'd rather imitate each other.
That's why life is so boring because
A.) no one is doing anything unique
B.) all we see is reruns of the same thing but
amongst different people
C.) there is no real platform for the truly creative to
shine.
Therefore, we become misfits in a sea of imitations.
This alone is a grave limitation to our potential.
A misfit should not be ashamed.
It is actually if they remain
On the course of achieving their full potential they
rise to fame, not just any fame but well-earned
fame with good intention.
Because they know what it took to grow over time
as a flower awaiting its blossoming.

None would notice the seed regardless of where it is planted until it begins to grow
Even then they are often neglected until the earth lends a hand.
There is an abundance of seeds waiting to grow.
The only problem is once they sense a quickly growing tree emerge their chemistry switches to that of a weed,
Clinging to the early riser so that they may feed off of said success.
Weeds are critically defined as an invasive species, edible, and can only be destroyed by the root.
It's odd to see a field of weeds and only one rose in the mix.
Imagine a forest with one tree covered in weeds and mushrooms sucking on its nutrients.
What are we taking from others pursuing their growth?
Do we not understand that a tree has branches that naturally grow leaves that fall into our hands as instruction to plant more
Seeds.
They need help to grow which means we have to be watered but if we can only see one tree, would we rather cut it down or let it grow?
A tree all alone in the midst of weeds.
Misfits are those trees struggling to grow because around them all they see are weeds stripping at their roots.
Our cries as outliers are hardly heard because truthfully we are suffocating.

The room for our exposure is closing tighter and tighter around our necks
Refusing to allow us to breathe.
Have you ever heard anyone speak of how restrained they felt to the point where they broke down in tears
claiming and expressing all their fears
Because they feel they cannot breathe.
This is why so many people quit early
Because they can't see that small hole waiting for them to emerge.
It's no easy feat.
Even the bravest flowers struggle to grow.
Just like the greatest rhythms and flows
Have to undergo
Reengineering but if they remain the same
They would remain cold and as lifeless as stone.
They are the greatest because they are unique
Not because they're the same as everyone else's
But because they were smelted under different circumstances
Called growth and development.
Not copy and paste it
The truth of the matter is we'll never reach our true height of effectiveness
If we stand by and wait for others to notice it.
How willingly are we going to step out of the pack
And take a chance to evolve.
We are better together for what we each can offer individually.
If we all copy each other because we're afraid to stand out

Where would we grow?
How afraid are we of a label?
It is not uncommon that we are quick to pin them
but slow to accept them.
It's easy to pin the tail on the donkey until you
realize someone is doing the same to you.
That's why the process is done blindly
Don't mind me but isn't it odd how
We'll do anything to fit in
But hate it when we're singled out?
The reason we should be accepted is because of
who we are
Not because of what we can copy.
That process is nothing but sloppy.
Our lives are so precious it pains me to see so
many people throw their life away to be accepted.
Truth be told this is the reason we're so separate.
We're Fighting for the wrong kind of acceptance.
Can we not accept ourselves for who we are?
Can we not see labels as just labels instead of
lifestyles?
Can we not understand the severity of our
purpose?
What's more, is that not a lot of us actually think of
such.
Fame has become the misfit's way of hiding who
they are as an authentically unique person.
Fame is easy to obtain these days because all you
have to do for the most part is play monkey see
monkey do.

Not that anyone is a monkey but it's the concept of the game to be exactly like the person in front of you.
How many of us lose ourselves to conformity?
How many of us are afraid to be ourselves?
Are *you* afraid?
Fear is the curtain misfits use to cover their desire to be free.
It's hard to be accepted and free at the same time
Most of the time it's one or the other
African Americans fought for freedom and peace yet they were segregated
Americans fought for freedom
They too were disowned by their predecessors.
Jesus fought for souls and peace
Yet he was crucified.
It was not because they wanted to be like everyone else, that they fought.
They understood what it meant to stand out
But they also knew that they had a voice because of it.
Would you rather accept your differences and make a difference or be like everyone else and be forgotten?
There's a reason why when one piece of bread spoils
The rest follow its suit.
Each slice is of the same loaf
And so each picks up the same strand of mold at the end of their shelf life.
A tree full of invasive bugs will not last long and must be chopped down,

Whereas if there were more trees, they'd protect each other.
If you had the power to change the course of your family lineage for the better
Would you?
If you could inspire someone just by being you
Would you?
Who would you mold yourself into to live the life you want?
What do you want?
Who do you want to be?
Misfits have a hard time accepting themselves because no one around them will do it for them
Isn't it hard to be alone?
I know what it's like to sit by myself with no one to talk to
I know what it's like to have an idea no one cares about
I know what it feels like to "fit in" but feel out of place at the same time.
I know what it's like to be lost in myself stressing over things in which I could not control.
Who would accept me for me if I could not do it for myself first?
I know what it feels like to hate myself because no one would talk to me first.
I was normal yet I was weird
I was cool yet I was isolated
Do you know what it feels like when people act like they care for you and turn on you the instant you show your true colors?

As bright as they may be, one could easily be
forsaken.
Why not be you initially and find the way to your
own heart?
We fight because we are hurting inside
Because there's a simple tear between who
We are and what "they" want us to be.
Everyone is a misfit in their own right.
Rumor has it
It's easy to lose sight
Of the things in which we find delight.
When the reason we fight is to be accepted.
So far gone is the nation of misfits, at least
The ones who seek change.
A group of people who wish to do more
Than what the average person would do
To make a difference.
The funny thing is to make a difference you
Have to be different.
The key to it all is accepting who we are.
We have to stop paying rent on everyone else's
lives
And live our own to thrive and offer the most we
can to ensure this world.
There is no need for shady blinds
When misfits get together.
There's a whole new atmosphere to the weather
When dreamers click play because
Others will see and join the way as themselves.
How can we submit to conformity,
When freedom sees
That the key to our full most fulfilling future

Is in the depths of the sea of our hearts?
Life is a journey we all must embark upon
Everyone has their own story
From the beginning
To the middle
To the end
The fillers
Thrillers
And killers
The mysteries
Romances and history
The unimaginable is possible
If only we'd step out of the crowd
And had hope that more existed.
To what are we enlisted?
Whose war are we fighting
When the most important battle is within ourselves
first.
Imagine a sky full of stars
Would it not be wonderful to see each star shine
purposefully alone?
Of course, because a sky with one star alone is
only seen in the morning
and seldom appreciated.
It is of its own constellation but we only accept it for
a season.
Constellations are more attention-grabbing
Because they cause us to wonder.
Wonder,
This term is rarely said anymore because it seems
like everything is already figured out.
I wonder why that is?

I wonder what it would be like if we could see those
windows of distant opportunity.
It's one thing to do things quickly
But what comes fast goes fast.
What comes with time stays over time.
Yet it's hard to fit in with a group of stars that you
aren't supposed to be with.
If the big dipper had ten extra stars would it be the
big dipper?
If there were a hundred north stars
Would there be such a thing?
Be free to be you.
Be free to be different.
Be a bold misfit because the only *person* you need
to aspire to be like is you.

~THE WORLD'S ACCEPTANCE~

This isn't the first time acceptance has been
mentioned.
It's the plague of today,
The silent epidemic,
That so many of us are willing to kill ourselves for
The disease known as, lack of self
How hard is it to look in the mirror and see that you
shine?
Some of us have a hard time making eye contact
with ourselves yet we love attention from others.
The world accepts those who wish to help
But it is flooded with so much selfishness
That we can only see the world as a leech
Sucking at all positive determination
And growth amongst those who wish for more.
We think people are good because they donate

No, it's the reason why you help that makes the difference.
Hope is fading further and further into the distance
This world accepts the oddballs of life
That have the potential to make life easier.
Society is oftentimes referred to in the bible and churches,
As the world.
If you noticed I refer to the world as it is
And society as it is also.
The world is being polluted by society's notion of what it should be like.
Society is overrun by what?
A darkness that we can't see
Because we've turned a blind eye
To the crime scenes
Of dreams
Of rising kings
And queens
Human beings
Who just want to live.
How many of us just wanna live?
Nowhere seems safe until
We find a way to feel safe
Through acceptance.
Commonality
The state of sharing features or attributes.
We often try to find what we have in common with everyone.
It's easy to accept the things we don't feel the need to hide.

It's easier to subside than to realize that we'd be
accepted more for our minor but significant
differences
In the existence of abstract instances.
Every story has its own protagonist
One who finds the key to their existence
Through plot.
What is the plot of our lives that they should merge
With everyone else's in tandem.
A story that tells the same tale
Over the course of a thousand books is always
Interpreted in a new frame of reality.
An altered formality
That's accepted by readers near and far.
What is acceptance?
Acceptance is the action or process of being
received as adequate or suitable, typically to be
admitted into a group.
What is the price of such a thing?
Your freedom?
Your hopes?
Your dreams?
Your ideas?
Who you are as a whole?
What are you doing trying to be received by others
like a dollar when you are worth much more.
Why must we pay millions of dollars worth of our
soul for a cent of acceptance?
This world, this society today is hell-bent on being
Suitable to everyone else's expectations.
Are our own expectations not high enough for our
attention?

Maybe not, maybe we should start expecting more of ourselves so that when others try to pressure us we already know what we're capable of and have long since been pursuing.
We shouldn't be strangers to our capabilities waiting for a group to see.
It's not like they are the ones with the key
To what drives you.
It's crazy how sometimes scribbles come forth as the most brilliant form of art.
It's the eyes of the outside world that binds us inside.
They scramble our lines waiting for them to crumble.
If someone saw a picture of scribbles as scribbles
Are they truly looking at the art?
Sometimes paintings, drawings, writings
Are created with errors to add emphasis to the intended perspective.
But it's often found that "perfection" is more acceptable.
Flawless is the pardon of lawlessness
Why?
If you look a certain way you could get away with murder
If you walk a certain way you can get admitted sooner.
The eyes are the windows to the soul
But also the prison that holds a thousand others.
How are we looking at people, each other?
Are we assessing each other's flaws without understanding the depth they inspire?

Are we glaring at their past as if it doesn't matter
As if their presence couldn't be changed because
of it?
What is it that we are holding onto that is
restraining us from accepting ourselves?
The eyes of those around us are not always
watching for our wellbeing but our downfall as well.
Not every foot will turn to rush to the rescue when
we need it.
Even amongst those we trust and put all our hope
into to be by our side in our present time of need.
The people who accept us, how soon would it be if
you made a change that set you apart would you
be cast aside?
What are we trying to earn in a crowd that we
cannot earn when looking in the mirror?
It's like we are inviting the chains of emptiness to
envelope our hearts because we are afraid of
whether or not who we are is valuable enough to be
accepted,
Acknowledged,
Memorable,
Noticeable,
What is it?
Why must we be valued by everyone else when we
don't even understand our own worth half of the
time?
This is especially prevalent in the younger
population.
Worth is defined by everything besides what we
say about ourselves.
It's like the image we see in the mirror is not valid.

A lot of us feel empty and wouldn't dare admit it
Because the minute that happens
There goes the clique.
There go your friends
There goes the image you worked so hard to build
That wasn't even your own.
If it was your own it wouldn't matter
Because once the glass over their eyes shatters
They'll see you for you and even if they leave
It won't matter because you were real.
Artificial is never as good as the real thing.
As much as we try and engineer things
To be better than the natural
We cannot excel what was made perfect the way it
was.
The thing is that instead, we try to add and subtract
what we want in order to fit the mix.
It's like talking about left and right Twix
They're the same thing yet they feud.
We are fighting ourselves to feel worthy of
ourselves
In order to be purchasable by the general public.
We could be a jet yet we toss ourselves into
Walmart like toys.
Are we not cutting ourselves short by hiding behind
the curtains of our reality?
At the end of the day, who do you have to deal
with?
You.
How intentional are we on being ourselves
Before we are clouded with the thoughts of what
everyone else wants is to be?

It's hard to push when everything is pulling you
back.
We ostracize ourselves to fit in, doing things to
spite others or our upbringing
Because we think that that is who we are
Without realizing that being different isn't the act of
changing who you are to please or spite someone.
You aren't who you think you are.
What are you hiding?
Why are you hiding?
You, we've got to break the shells around our
hearts molded by everyone else's agenda.
Are we not the potter of our own mindset?
Unless a claim is beneficial and of value, we
shouldn't hold onto it.
To be different by default, each one of us is special.
It just takes a personal eye to realize it.
Acceptance only lasts but a second
Just like the passing seasons
And the rain
And time
And the sun's time in our windows
And the moon at night
And our lives.
We cannot create and live in unacceptable things
And claim that they are right because you have a
group.
You don't want people to force things upon you yet
you do it to establish power for what you know is
wrong to be acceptable in the sight of man.
What do you want?
To be seen?

Noticed?
Unprescribed?
Worthy of a subscribe?
Where do we pin the total worth of our lives?
If I'm being honest there is a lot to think about when
it comes to trying to live in the heads of others.
Sometimes I wonder why people would fight for me.
Why I'd fight for them.
Is it because I wanted their validation
Or because they wanted mine?
Is there ever going to be a just because or an that's
just how I am?
The more we learn ourselves the more we realize
that when we fight for others out of pure intention
Rather than their undivided attention
We'd be much more satisfied.
There's no reason to hide that part of yourself that
holds good intentions.
We shouldn't feed ourselves off of useless
attention.
It's like trapping ourselves in detention.
Not to mention that there is more to life than being
accepted.
Sometimes we have to be redirected
Because our reason is what matters more than
anything else.
Our why is the key to the hole gaping in our hearts.
We must accept ourselves before anyone will
acknowledge us.
That's the only way we can be satisfied with
ourselves whether or not we are perfect or
imperfect in everyone else's eyes.

This world is the same
It is a home meant to harbor the light even in times
of darkness.
We have to accept the fact that even in the darkest
tunnels there is a light to signal the exit.
Look inside the tunnel of your heart
Look through your own two eyes in the mirror and
see
That the light at the end of the tunnel resides
In deep
No longer fight to be accepted
Fight because that's just how you are.
Be you and you'll be recognized
Acceptance is fleeting because it expects
stagnation.
You are ever-changing and growing
Don't halt to be acceptable in everyone else's sight.
If anything, work to be acceptable in your creator's
sight, God.
Men die
Women die
We all die.
Acceptance only lasts for a short period of time,
don't get stuck living for it.

~THE WORLD'S FAME~

With fame comes a lot of baggage.
You're always being watched
There is no freedom behind the scenes.
What we would do for fame is much more
infiltrating.
We would rather lose ourselves for quick
gratification.

Fame has its pros
Fame has its cons.
A very small number of us achieve fame by our
own abilities.
We limit our strength to be like the others.
So what is the price of fame?
There is much to lose
And there is some to gain.
Temporary,
But exciting in its own way.
The attention one receives in the eyes of the world,
can shape and change people.
Acceptance and fame operate hand and hand.
Fame is the result of acceptance by a growing
number of people.
The price of fame and of acceptance are similar.
Fame costs more for the man who seeks only
acceptance.
Acceptance is cheap to one who does things out of
love.
Fame and acceptance are hard to uphold in the
world today because you must transform to the
ideals of the crowd.
Your thoughts and ideas may become invaluable.
You don't decide what you do if you are bound by
the acceptance aspect of fame.
Love is the ongoing topic of this book,
Tying itself into every fraction of life's challenges.
It is the reason why we choose
Certain instances over others
Why we do certain things before we do anything
else.

When it comes to fame, it determines the direction
And creation of our content.
You know,
what the audience eats,
Sits for hours on end to enjoy,
Tells their friends about,
Walks to,
Lives by,
Accepts as a part of their lives,
This is the inside of the outside.
There are pros and cons to everything that we do.
What gets famous gets press.
Press means attention.
It turns our heads
It triggers our desire
What that desire may be,
I couldn't tell you.
Everyone at some point wants to be recognized,
Noticed in a flash, like we mean the world.
It would be lovely to feel valued at such a wide
expanse.
Fame is a short topic because it's explained
indirectly on a constant basis.
It ties into what we'd be willing to do to be
accepted,
Where we put our attention,
And how we carry ourselves whether it be out of
greed or humility,
How we treat our relationships, our kin,
And whether we choose to love or hate.
Believe it or not, hatred is more famous than love.

It's not rare that love is overshadowed by the thought of hate.
Hate is like an epidemic when love is like the obvious cure that rarely if ever gets similar interest.
The followers of that movement have greatly declined to bitterness.
I could make a list of the things that get the spotlight before love.
It's simple
Look at your phone.
Look at your TV
when we see it it's only for a short minute
And then an afterthought.
Fame is not for all of us.
We live in a cruel world where everything and everyone is not created and automatically considered equal.
What you may seek vs the next man/woman could be way different.
Fame comes with a lot of eyes,
Reporters and cameras floating around like flies,
Your face is on signs,
You'll be constantly criticized.
Truth be told it'd be fine,
If some of us were prepared for it.
If we go out seeking fame
it'll hit us in an odd way
What I mean is that once you get it
That desire shifts quickly and is not the same.
Being famous can get annoying after a while.

The only time it doesn't phase certain people is
when they do what they love and for the people
they love.
If as I said earlier you do what you do for attention
Eventually, that grows stale.
Everything around you will indefinitely grow pale.
What is fame in this world?
I couldn't tell you
It depends solely on the person seeking it
Or who just so happens to stumble upon it.
Fame is a two-faced con artist depending on who it
encounters.
The world is most famous for the beauty it beholds
But when it has issues no one seems to care.
How often do celebrities cry alone?
Feeling like if anyone knew,
They'd lose their hard-earned throne?
Some of them just want to be human
But with all eyes on them, it's hard for them to live a
normal *human* life.
It's as if we put the constraint of perfection on those
who have attained favor in the eyes of man.
Is it not human to make mistakes?
Don't we all, or is it because we aren't in the
spotlight that it doesn't matter?
There's another point.
Those of us who claim we don't want fame,
are not better than those who live in it.
If they went around forcing their agenda on you
how would you feel?
It's not like they go out of their way each day to
make you feel inferior.

If you don't like that kind of attention, leave it there.
Too many times do people try to bite those who
worked hard on what they LOVED and rose to
honest fame.
We can't keep trying to drag people into the
shadows.
Which raises the question,
Why do we try so desperately to paint a bad image
of those who people look up to, are inspired by, and
watch regularly?
Is it to boost our own views?
If so I'll say it now, gossip is just the conversation of
leeches.
What else are you doing besides trying to divert the
light off of someone to shine it on yourself.
Now if they did something horrendous then by all
means expose it.
But if they're in a simple romantic relationship
Leave the people alone.
Privacy is still a courtesy
But for some reason, those who rise to fame don't
get any of that.
There's so much crap in the world that's why
We need new light,
People who will step into the light and extend a
hand to the people without concern for the public
eye's view.
charity/good tidings is a sign of character,
Don't make it a stunt to gain supporters.
We rarely get to see how famous people let alone
people in general really help out in the world
around them.

Where there is bad there is good but we,
unfortunately, gravitate towards the bad.
So, what is fame?
Is it a blessing or a curse?
Couldn't tell you…
The world we live in is too sporadic to tell such a
thing,
It's all up for interpretation.
This is why love is the key to a fulfilling life whether
publicity rises or dips, whether people realize your
name or not, whether millions recognize your name
or face at any given moment or not.
Love nullifies anything that would penetrate the
desire to move.
Don't stop moving because the following slows
down.
Don't stop moving because people don't
understand you.
Don't stop moving when you feel all alone.
Be beyond a trend,
And ascend above your own expectations.
Fame is but a luxury blended in a curse of reach
and significance.

~THE WORLD'S FORTUNE~

Fortune and worth.
What are such things to a man?
What are such things that differ from wealth and
luxury?
What is material that cannot be interpreted as
internal?
We always look at the outside but we rarely look at
the substance within.

We see a diamond is found in a mess of rocks
Yet we only highlight the diamond after it's cut.
Fortune and worth,
The section is only titled fortune,
chance, or luck as an external, arbitrary force
affecting human affairs.
First, we'll strip it down to chance.
Chances are chances but chance is an undefined
outcome.
It makes certain things...
Invigorating.
What I mean is, there is the fact that there can be a
sliver of hope in any situation.
When we are hopeful it makes everything around
us seem worth enduring
Because of a slight possibility.
This world is full of chances and opportunities,
If we'd move we'd find them.
What I mean by move is that we need to take the
idea of chance and run with it.
Do something with that hope.
There's no use of hope if it's just going to sit.
We love the idea of chances but we leave it at that,
An idea...
Ideas remain ideas unless they're brought to reality,
If you read a mystery novel you'll learn that the idea
of possibility is used to make you think critically
about every plausible outcome
Backed by evidence.
A lot of the evidence in our cases is simple.
To put it in perspective, think about if-then
statements.

If I do this, that will happen (probably)
Nothing in life is guaranteed.
That is why we must move regardless of the initial
outcome.
That's when if thens become this, then next
statements.
If I do this, then that will happen but whether what I
want or don't want to happen, happens, next I will
in order to make such happen.
We give up too easily because the opportunity of
chance often seems transparent,
See-through, untouchable.
(If you think you'll get away with something wrong,
forget about what I said because you will be taken
down by life, evil only prevails for a season before it
is destroyed either by the hand of life or the law.)
But although opportunity and chance seem out of
reach
If we reached, we'd see how easily we could touch
it.
Most instances of fortune are the stems of winning.
In a sense, it is winning but we often think about
game shows, lottery, gambling, etc.
In my sense winning is finally realizing the results of
one's labor.
Then chance loses its flavor and lessons take root.
You no longer chase the chance but the lessons.
One learns through the movement towards that
which they hope for, making it into reality.
What I mean by this is that while we learn,
a possibility can build credibility in you to make
what you want into a reality.

We have a lot of chances in life
And as chance would have it,
 we have a lot of opportunities available to us.
This is no secret.
We've got to move.
There is no such thing as luck
Only trial and error and trial again.
Repeat.
Sometimes coincidence happens but even so, it
happens according to a coordinated sequence of
events whether planned or unplanned.
As it stands, what we get is the result of our action.
The world is full of chances
And chance just so happens to be at the end of
each of those.
There is a chance to change the world for better,
There is a chance to destroy it altogether
The thing is this world is fragile
And our accumulative choices have an effect.
And as luck would have it the world complies but
the result isn't always the best.
In its definition, Fortune emphasizes external affairs
What about internal affairs?
How does fortune affect us on the inside?
What is the side effect of the idea of luck and
chance?
Like I said earlier, it depends on what you do with
such things.
Human affairs
Are interactions and relationships that just are
affected also because of such.
If you move you may lose people

If you move people may come
If you move you may find yourself in that sliver of
hope.
If you never move you won't know.
That's the internal effect the idea of fortune has on
one, it makes one think ahead
And it spins the thread
of uncertainty that tests your faith.
We wonder offhandedly, what would happen if the
ideal result didn't happen?
But what if that result just so happens to come to
pass?
Wouldn't there be a different internal reaction?
It depends on what you took a chance on.
Your dream
Your life
Your goals
Your spirituality
Your faith.
Whatever it is think about it like this,
Fortune is not the money you can gain in an instant
But the power of credibility learned through trial and
error and next. Lessons are more valuable than a
piece of paper that buys you things.
And imagine yourself on a cliff; you can either jump
and embrace the water below
Or play it safe and never witness the thrill of flying.
In regards to this world's current state
We need to take a chance on making it a better
place because chances are

There are two outcomes of our labors as a collective

1.) Our kids live in a world full of hate and of little hope and faith in the uncertain factors of life and opportunities don't exist for those who wish for positive influence.
2.) Our kids embrace a world of hope and opportunity. Inspiration and growth is the lesson of hardship, not hatred, and spite. A world of peace.

Fortune isn't made, it's earned.
Move with what you want to pursue,
The only way you'll know the outcome is if you go.
The truth is you miss 101% of the shots you don't take,
That extra percent is the energy you spent running away from your opportunity trying to escape.
Fortune is not the world's but ours to embrace.

~THE HAPPINESS OF THIS WORLD~

What is happiness?
What makes one happy?
What generates such feelings?
There are a multitude of factors that induce happiness,
But from what I've heard
It doesn't last long.
A lot of things only last for a second.
But if only for a second we'd embrace such luxuries, who knows what might happen.
Happiness is a luxury that a lot of us take for granted.

Granted it sneaks up on us and runs away fast depending on our lifestyle.

There are a lot of things in this world that strip happiness away and are highlighted almost religiously.

I've mentioned the light frequently throughout this book and for some, its idea acts as a hook for hope.

Hope is the precursor of happiness

Because hope encourages the souls of those who seek more.

Have you ever had high hopes for a movie and it exceeded such expectations?

How happy were you or were you mildly impressed?

Happiness is a moment that remembers itself.

The happiness of this world would come from a multitude of things.

Peace

Tranquility

Unity

Patience amongst men and women.

But is happiness sufficient when it comes to material things?

The happiness of this world does not exist.

How can a world that is presently being torn apart be happy?

It's not even the physical world A.K.A the Earth that I'm talking about.

I'm talking about society

And this has been the main topic in this book's entirety

wrapped around the topic of the world like skin.
In church, you'd often hear a speaker mention "the world"
What they mean is the vanities of society.
There are quite a few that don't need to be mentioned because anyone reading already knows what they are off the top of their head.
Happiness could be eternal but in our present world
Yet there is hardly any room for it to spring forth as it was intended.
It's not a feeling or emotion that purposefully hides from us.
It's one we have to step outside of our dark-filled comfort zones to embrace.
See here's the thing, a lot of our comfort zones are just bins of darkness
And trust me
The dark does not appeal to the light.
Happiness doesn't come without a price
As most things don't,
It requires genuine work and effort,
Persistence and drive,
Motivation and grit.
Sure a moment can make you happy for that present day
But how long is that present-day compared to the abundance of others to follow if granted?
A lot of people waver between
Happy and sad
Depressed and motivated
Anxious and confident
Like a pendulum on a clock.

It won't stop unless something about it changes.
It's hard to embrace what is unfamiliar,
Kids these days especially are more prone to
depression than ever before
Maybe because when they look at the score
Of likes follows and shares
It seems like no one even cares
Sometimes parents aren't even aware
And when someone lashes out,
The argument's never fair.
What makes someone happy
Beyond the extent of dopamine?
I understand it's the chemical behind the scenes
But happiness isn't just a feeling.
If one would embrace it they'd see it's a mindset
Bred by freedom.
There's a reason why kids are afraid of the dark,
Because monsters lurk
In its shadowy corner.
We face them every day without even realizing it.
Jealousy
Envy
Hatred
Strife
Lasciviousness
The list goes on but even the darkest person
couldn't name them all.
Not all of them are visible through everyone's eyes.
Pain and suffering lurk around every corner even in
the light
Except somehow someway the light tends to
weaken such instances.

We've strayed from happiness,
The state of being happy,
Feeling or showing pleasure or contentment
But excruciatingly hard to embrace.
The idea sounds nice,
As most ideas do to the ear of those who listen,
Though it is evident that a plethora of ideas are
cast aside and forgotten.
It's not a rare occurrence.
In fact, it's the most common occurrence in today's
society.
People throw who they are away for the portrayed
appearance of happiness and success.
Sometimes the things we advertise are their own
con artists,
audiences are quickly cheated into losing
themselves in the pursuit of something that may
never make them feel fulfilled or happy.
We, as we are the world
Are tearing ourselves apart chasing idealistic
illusions.
Happiness is attainable to all
But it is avoided by many who
Don't wish to change,
Refuse to accept it,
Or stray from it entirely
In pursuit of a momentary dose.
What makes you happy?
Not what tricks you into thinking you're happy
What makes you genuinely want to move forward in
life?
What is worth the struggle?

Are you willing to step outside of the darkness to embrace the wonders of the light on the other side?
This means setting aside drugs
Fornication (sex outside of marriage)
Jealousy
Envy
Adultery (cheating on your wife/husband)
All of these things and a long list of others
Are falsified instances of happiness/fulfillment.
Set aside revenge
And hate
Anger and pride
Selfishness
And the desire of the flesh.
Happiness is only fleeting when the presence of darkness overshadows the very presence of your heart.
Imagine how dark the world would have to be for happiness not to exist.
Take a look around and you'll see it's getting close.
There will be a moment in everyone's life to choose between light and dark
True and false,
Beginning and end.
The choice will always be ours to make
That's the beauty of life,
Even when we are bound
We always have a choice unless we strip it away from ourselves or someone else.
Consequences don't exist for nothing,
And it's no wonder there is little instance of uplifting

In this world, or as one of the greatest television shows says, "this accursed world"
What's our mode of change?
Happiness is sought but seldom found by those with ill intention and practice toward themselves or others.
The happiness of this world does not exist unless things change.

~THE SADNESS OF THE WORLD~

Is the most common attraction amongst humans today.
It has a way of dragging even the best people down into the depths of stagnation and emptiness.
It's easy to lose sight of oneself when everyone else around you is blind as well.
Sadness has a way of clouding one's vision of themselves
And everything around them.
It adds depth to the darkness.
Now before I go in deeper, some instances and events should induce such a feeling,
Like funerals, the loss of someone close
And other events that would hold such a weight on one's soul.
There are occasions where such events stir up extra emotions,
Like hate
Disbelief
Etc.
It happens to the best of us.
Pain is unavoidable in life,

But as I said, sadness can quickly go from an
honest emotion
To the depth of the darkness.
Fuel if you will.
It is a feeling that can make one feel empty,
As if there is no vitality within their fleshly vessel.
Sadness stemming from loss is especially
Responsible for such occasions.
It's so common that you'll hear more about how sad
someone is over how happy they are.
There's nothing wrong with expressing how you
feel
Matter of fact it is healthy to respectfully express
your feelings,
There is a need for support in this world that is
seldom offered
And rarely accepted.
Looking into it at a time like this,
With the world in turmoil due to pandemic and other
factors of life
It's dire.
With so much light-heartedness, you'd think people
would move to know themselves.
Not so.
Most if not some have resorted to sulking behind a
screen.
The thought of less is easier to comprehend than
the idea of more.
Sadness is the light-hearted version of depression,
It's actually considered a symptom.
There are a host of triggers for this feeling
And it acts as a leech

Sucking away at the lifeline of hope that few of us hold dear.

It's a slow process that is hardly recognizable until it has dealt its final blow.

This world is covered in it.

In the worst-case scenarios, this feeling has grown into depression

And has furthered itself into hatred

And further unto death.

It has the ability to stick and hold until it is Resisted with love.

So many people live in their despair and sorrow that surprisingly enough, small occurrences strike like a wrecking ball in the lives of many people, Tossing them meters back into darkness.

The hatred I mentioned earlier isn't necessarily fixated on another person all the time

In many cases, the real hate is directed at the person that is portrayed in the mirror.

Sadness is not a joke

And it is not a friend

It is not something to be suppressed and hidden

It is not something gutted out alone.

Tears will fall in its presence

Weakness will spring in its arrival.

Those things are better than leaving with it clinging to your house (your soul)

Let it go.

Some events may be harder to let go but they are easy to replay over and over again.

Our world THIS world is littered with crumbling houses.

And the rubble has polluted this earth
Offering darkness as the only cure to such pain.
Escaping is all some people think they can do
Run and run and run and never face the problem.
Change doesn't happen by running away all of the
time.
Life is never going to be a perfectly straight line
There will be hiccups
And hicdowns
Extremely fulfilling highs
And excruciatingly painful lows.
How many of us are willing to rise up and let go?
Tell someone how we feel instead of allowing a
screen to rule your heart's emotions.
How many of us are brave enough to allow
ourselves to cry in the arms of someone who
cares?
How many of us dare to allow anyone else to care?
Who among us will lead the movement of
openness?
Doors have to fall for change to occur.
Chains have to be loosed for darkness to shatter.
There is too much darkness in this world for us not
to see the sliver of light still hanging on to offer us
its hand.
We have to move beyond ourselves and open up,
we can't hide from ourselves any longer
Because whose hand will we die by but our own?
This is today's problem
In which the only solution rests in every one of us
individually.
We don't know who we are anymore

We struggle with our worth because we allow
everyone else to determine it for us.
We were all born for a reason
And we all leave for the same.
Sadness will no longer hold down the ranks of
those who wish to shine with the fullness of their
hearts.
Darkness will not prevail in the eyes of those who
reach out and lend a hand to others out of love.
There is no escape from change,
It'll either slither into the dark
Or it will claw its way into the light.
Strange how one has to fight harder than the other
to make a difference in this world.
The change starts within us and if we keep allowing
the enhancer of the darkness to strip our hearts of
hope
Then we'll only fall deeper and deeper into the
given abyss of emptiness.
Sadness is not the only culprit,
Pride also holds such weight,
Lust also,
Maliciousness,
Drunkenness,
Witchcraft
Hatred
Variance
Idolatry
Wrath
Strife
Seditions
Heresies

Envyings
Murders
Revellings
And the list goes on
These are all unclean and adopted practices
amongst man.
Each one has its own unique quality of dragging us
down.
A lot of us live in them unable to escape because
They give us what?
The instant gratification of pleasure.
It's a quick "remedy" for sorrow
According to the chemicals altered in our brains.
The problem is
Eventually more and more and more will be
required to quell the pains of yesterday.
There are alternative options that
Are easily adoptable
But seldom admonished.
We are social beings who no longer know how to
communicate,
We can't talk about how we feel because we are
Burning inside with the fear of being judged,
My question is why do we judge each other for
being human.
It's like we hate the fact that we exist,
Truth be told we've been trying to replace ourselves
for years,
Robots have no emotion
Self-driving systems have no eyes
But we rely on them more than we rely on the fact
that we have each other.

Look into it and you'd see that the world's sadness lies in all the hearts of those who don't care to be heard.
Why sink when somewhere there's a hand to pull you out of the darkness.?
There's always a way if you look for it.
Too bad giving up seems like the common option spreading around the world.
Escaping can't be an option either,
Letting go is the only way relief can be instilled and last.
no one is a stranger to pain and sorrow
There's always help especially in the time of dire need.
People care,
Reach out beyond your pit of comfort and climb to the freedom your heart seeks.
We'd never know it unless our heart cried out for us when we can do nothing but bottle up and cry.
Sadness is the increaser of the dark,
But it is not rare for a blind man to scope his surroundings with his hands until he finds the handhold he's looking for to guide him.
Sadness occurs even in the light
But the object of motion is making the decision
Between living in it
Or accepting its departure and moving on.
Regardless of how hard it can be sometimes,
That is why we must seek help in times like these.
Our world is a reflection of our being
If we aren't helping ourselves and each other do better

Then how much are we really helping this world heal?
The sadness of this world is spreading at an Astronomical rate,
It starts with opening up our heart's gates that we can de-escalate the tyranny of the dark.
Envelope this world with kindness and extend a hand,
One does not have to do anything grand to help someone on their knees stand.
Because all it requires is a hand,
That hand does not always have to be physical though,
Words have the power to uplift just as much as they do to destroy,
Prayer works whether you believe in it or not,
It works.
Just being around as a genuine friend works.
It never hurts to ask questions because
Sometimes all someone needs is someone to listen,
An ear goes a long way.
Sometimes tears can touch the soul of someone who truly cares.
Care
Where is the care in this world?
I love the phrase 'I don't care"
The reason I love it is because it can be taken several ways.
It can be dismissive
Defensive
Offensive

And counteractive.
People say it all the time without realizing the
impact it has on the receiving end.
Sometimes when I was young and would get into
an argument
I could never defend myself because I am not a
good arguer
I prefer to abstain from that pain that others view as
luxury.
Whenever I'd get offended or backed into a corner,
the only phrase I could grasp on to was "I don't
care."
Imagine someone told you they hated you and they
didn't mean it but you out of rage said that phrase,
You'd have no idea how much that hurt them,
And you'd be stuck wallowing in your
despair until one of you two admits the fault.
Sadness stems from so many situations it's
disgusting.
And if no one cared it would only breed and spread
deeper and deeper into our cores.
This is why I say we need to step outside of
ourselves and actually "see" what's going on
around us.
The people dying,
The people suffering,
The people pleading for a chance,
Fighting for approval that'll only drag them deeper
into the dark
There is so much going on that we have become
blind to ourselves.

This is why stories are important because if no one shared their story
No one would be moved.
Closing this sect I recently came across a text I wrote back in April and it goes as such
"From beginning to end, a story unfolds.
Crevices of a man or woman quickly unfold
Things you couldn't see before are revealed.
The hardest part about telling one's story is facing the demons of times passed.
No one can face them except the person that endured the pain and hardship of that life.
We are birthed with the bread of opportunity
Yet the Devil is coward enough to steal candy
From a baby,
Our youth is the most cumbersome
Because at the time it is hard to delegate good from evil, scolding from hate;
The hypersensitivities of youth are what the Devil tries to utilize to keep us down.
We can not submit.
Every detail of your life matters,
Otherwise, your story would never unfold with the power it needs.
The world will know your silence when they hear your voice.
When the time comes, I command you to speak.
Be prepared to tell all who wish and would hate to know, because what people need most is someone who knows.
5:55 am 4/29/21"

~WORLD PEACE?~

Imagine a world where people didn't war out of
pride
It's easy to envision but hard to believe as possible.
It isn't but peace is only attainable through silence
and
Patience.
In this world, everyone has something different to
fight for,
Agreement will be the hardest thing to delve
People war over things like
sex/gender alteration (there are only 2 male and
female there's no room for argument: pointless)
Religion
Belief
Politics
Principle
Race (how long will it take us to realize we're all the
same race just different colors like crayons are all
crayons, just different colors, I don't see each
individual color packed in separate boxes.)
Societal standing
Culture
The list goes on.
The only things we seem to agree on are that we all
live (unless killed before birth) and we all die.
But even that is warred over pointlessly.
If there were a battle between the peace in this
world and the overwhelming unrest and
Hostile entities,
Peace would be eradicated.

Although this is going to be hit on further in the
following sections,
Social media is the catalyst of our peace's decay.
It strips our time, beckoning us to indulge in
pointless arguments to make ourselves feel
involved.
Negativity and propaganda is spreading like a
wildfire in such areas,
Everyone's eyes are glued to it.
It is said that if you want to know anything
Read a book.
No one wants to read these days because its
deemed "useless"
This is why a lot of people are not creative and are
not willing to attain new realms of knowledge or
permit their focus to diverge from the promises of
supposed prosperity.
All we are shown is highlights and dark lights.
More often than not we choose to digest the dark
lights and turn the highlights into envy poles.
We choose envy.
Envying leads to war also.
We're so caught up in what everyone else has
That we can't even see what we have right in front
of us.
This is why houses break down and divide
Because something as simple as a double-tap
holds all of the power.
We argue over pointless things that envy funnels
into much bigger things.

Listen if you're a wife, don't be out here trying to be like every other woman because if your husband loves you he chose you for you (the authentic you).
We catch ourselves comparing our stature to everyone else's,
robbing ourselves of time that is so precious.
It could be better used to build up a relationship with your present friends, family, and God
We are not present anymore.
And we are warring over highlights that only last for a second.
We fight over fleeting things.
Unnecessary things are hit upon more than the battle for change.
Warring always leaves one party happy and damaged and the other angry and damaged.
No one is ever complete after the war.
If you want to be heard, don't try and create something that you know will cause controversy.
Attention is not worth the hassle.
Yes we need to stand up for what is right
Like racist brutality
Sexual assault
And a load of other things,
The problem is we're repeating the past time and time again
And I know the whole world won't read this book, let alone a hundred people but
Why is it so hard for us to move on and away from these childish things?
We're so prideful it's sickening,
And as I said earlier this is a call to action.

When are we going to move away from the past
and move toward the future?
I believe it's possible
Because when peace lasts longer than anxiety
Unrest
Doubt
Pressure
Hatred
Strife
Envy
It truly becomes something beyond the beauty
Of what we can create.
We only highlight what's created but it's a slim
Chance that we'll find the things destroyed in the
process.
Now, let me ask you this,
Have you ever listened to a symphony in perfect
harmony?
It has the power to draw forth true emotion and
focus on the atmosphere,
It has the power to open us up when we least
expect it.
It's not the music that holds the power, but the
concept of diverse instruments coming together to
bring forth one result.
What result are we hoping to leave as a whole
when this world is destroyed?
Peace is so important to true growth.
Competition can thrive in peace because then
competitors understand the significance of learning
in a manner that doesn't spark unnecessary haste.
Copycat nature is beginning to raise war

This day because the true creators are blotted
By the crowd,
Never to get the recognition they earned.
Our world is like a puzzle missing a million pieces
because they fell off the table in one fell swoop of
frustration.
The world is only getting darker in these conditions.
See the light,
See it.
The light is calming but we are stuck being
comfortable where we are because we don't think
change is necessary,
It is necessary now more than ever,
Even years and years after this release date
It's inevitable
There is no escape.
We need to move toward the light and leave the
dark behind before it's past too late.
This world, us, *we* have had too many self-induced
breaks,
Tears,
And dislocations.
Take a vacation
of peace by stepping away
From the turmoil, this world is spiraling in.
Make a true dedication
to what puts us in a better location for peace.
How many of us today are locked in the dog pen of
untamed loose ends?
Peace
In our time would be
An astounding feat to behold.

Camaraderie,
Love,
Kindness towards others overflowing our lives.
I understand the whole world will not choose this way,
Because some of us are greedy.
Some of us are prideful.
Some of us are conceited.
Some of us are lost to what we really want out of life.
Some of us are too comfortable being stuck in a void of our own creation.
100% of anything is incomplete
There's a hole in every wall that you can't see.
I can't even see them and I'm looking at them.
Some could say world peace is unattainable
Unrealistic
And a vain movement,
They'd be correct because the entire world will not be at peace but that doesn't rule out a large portion that can be.
People who do not believe in the object of peace
Are usually the ones who refuse their input in the movement.
Is it a worthwhile battle?
It seems like in this world, everything rolls out to become a battle.
Sometimes it's with swords.
Sometimes with guns.
Then words,
Then bombs,
Then politics,

Then words again,
Then money,
And all of these things repeat themselves over and
over and over again.
What is enough or when are we ever going to get
enough of warring?
I'll tell you
We won't.
Not unless there is a shift in the majority.
100% world peace is unrealistic.
We all have access to the world in our hands for at
least 2-24 hours a day.
Take some time out and spread kindness
It's at least one step millions of people have a hard
time taking, that you can do to make a difference.
World peace?
We'll see.

~THE LIVES OF THIS WORLD~

There is an increasing number of us every day, yet
it is balanced by time.
There are countless lives lost,
A lot of misunderstood people who disappeared
Without a hint of their potential being
acknowledged,
Who lives in a world like this?
What is living?
Some would say
Money
Fame
Fortune
Living the "lavish" life is living.
Is it though?

After a while that kind of stuff gets old.
In high school, we live for "fun"
What fun is in those years
According to the archives of lives lost due to high
school fun
Are drugs
Parties
Sex
More drugs
Is that really fun or just destroying ourselves until
we feel we've escaped the stresses of life?
Life is stressful.
The corners,
The fields,
Wherever you go or try to hide,
Life will find a way to put something on you that will
test your strength.
How many of us would say we're strong?
A lot of us.
But what do we do to get strong?
How are we strong?
What do we do to avoid the/or face the pressures of
life?
drugs?
Parties?
Sex?
More drugs?
Or do we resort to other tactics like
Reading
Writing
Talking to people in a real manner
Opening up and seeking the proper help

Do we cry (there's nothing wrong with crying)
Do we pray
Do we look in the mirror
And say hey we gotta keep moving
Keep moving forward.
There are so many healthy opportunities but
A lot of us throw our lives away at the first sign of
adversity because it seems fun.
"It numbs the pain"
But it brings forth other pains as a result
"It helps me forget"
Once the moment is over then what?
It won't help you forget that it exists.
"I like it"
Say the same thing 10 years from now
And we'll see about that.
Sometimes "boring" is necessary for us to truly live.
A lot of us are living in the so-called "Now"
"Live in the moment"
Why live in a moment that only lasts for a second
that's not going to elevate me in any way shape or
form but kill me internally until I submit to the trials
of life trying to get right after I've already lost
myself?
Why would I waste my time earlier trying to run
away from what comes with living?
Hardship is a way to make us stronger but in
today's society
We take it as "oh well I'm not meant to be here
Life hates me,"
"I don't belong,"
"There's no point in trying to do better,"

"I'm too afraid,"
"That's scary,"
Change for the better is always going to be scary if
we live our lives running away from the issues that
we've been dealt with by our own hand.
Are we too afraid to face ourselves?
I'm curious as to what life would be like if we'd
extend ourselves and stretch away from anguish.
Peace requires silence,
Tranquility
Harmony, harmony, harmony
Sometimes we need to set this aside with a
pardoning,
A new form of bargaining
That doesn't cost our lives.
Sometimes it takes a host of hardship to reveal the
peace in the storm.
Every major storm has its eye.
Some of us are blazing the trail from the eye
straight into the thick of the headwinds that await us
In imbalance.
It's easy to stagger when we aren't balanced,
The scars remind me every day.
Sometimes it takes breaking to create room for an
awakening
But we can't run.
Either we face life as it is
Or we run from it and drown in its stronghold
Of trials without ever freeing ourselves from fear,
Anxiety,
Displacement,
And imbalance.

There are many ways to pursue a better path in preserving our lives.
I say this because every life matters in its own way
Regardless of skin color,
Gender (male or female),
Aspiration,
It does not matter because nothing happens by accident.
Understand this and move forward
The greatest asset you'll have outside of God,
Is yourself.
We have to take care of that person
Even when times get hard
To wallow in the dark is to encourage more darkness to spill into our souls.
We can't live in the things we can't control
That's why we need to make a conscious effort to protect our hearts, minds, and character
From the illusion of "fun"
When what we need especially at a young age
When pain hits just a little bit harder and
Running away and diving into the dark seems like the easy way out.
We've got to move and be intentional about our growth and leap outside of despair.
Be fair to yourselves.
Take an honest chance on your life.
If you get knocked on your butt a thousand times,
Pursue it to the one thousand one mark.
Our lives are too important to waste.
Rearrange your idea of fun and you will

See that fulfillment is much more valuable than a
moment that wastes you in an instant

~THE WORLD'S NEED TO BREATHE~

How many of us would say we are suffocating?
How many of us would say we can't breathe?
How trapped do you feel?
What's closing around your chest that just won't let
you go free?
I don't know
A lot of us are unknowingly claustrophobic to
isolation.
We can't operate on our own.
This isn't necessarily a bad thing
Because we aren't always the strongest on our
own.
It's not rare that we need help
The problem is it's hard for us to ask.
This world physically can't ask for our assistance
unless it forces our hand into action through
disaster.
We might make up the population of this world yet
we, although we have voices of some sort
Remain quiet when we need some help.
We know our own despair best
We know our pain
Or at least we should.
We need to breathe and as the last two sections
have been emphasizing the importance in
Self-accountability
And growth development.
Now it's embracing the relief.
Pressure is what causes suffocation

You can drown as I mentioned not too long ago
But you can also choke.
It could come upon you out of the blue.
We need room to breathe
It's like every around corner we turn
Someone
Or something
We don't know is breathing down our necks.
That's not a good feeling,
Perfectionism is not a good feeling.
Of course, people are going to be watching but
Sometimes we have to forget the crowd and slide
away for a moment.
If we struggle with isolation, don't be isolated
Isolate
Also known as taking time away from all the outside
noise.
This world is too loud.
Someone is always in someone's ear trying to force
an opinion.
Sometimes all someone wants is a moment even if
it lasts for a second
Of silence.
The power of silence is so immense that it
surprises me that it is a feared trait amongst
people.
Silence permits your ear to be tuned to the sound
of someone else's pain and affliction.
It makes you think more critically about your
surroundings.
It makes you observe.

It prepares our minds ahead of time and limits impulse.
So many arguments could be avoided if we learned to shut up and listen.
No man or woman is right all of the time
We need to learn what we can while we can.
Silence permits such information to be processed.
If we succumb to the noise
We shall surely
Disappear within it, losing ourselves in the process.
We need to breathe.
Our world needs to breathe.
It's suffocating in the filth we leave lying on the streets,
Water,
Environment,
And the atmosphere.
How can freedom be so easily cast aside by noise?
Because we've been blessed with a means to interpret it.
And we listen and we add
And add
And add
Like addition
Amongst millions
The subtraction is all the compounding
Compound thoughts that distort a plethora of finite principles.
Wearing a mask for years
Days
Hours
Even minutes

Is suffocating
And especially after the events in 2020
There's no way to forget the suffocating nature of
our lifestyles.
It's not just that year that had us suffocating.
Most of us were and are suffocating on the inside.
We're worried about things that are out of our
control like
Time.
We look at it anxiously and wonder whether or not
what we're doing with it is adequate to give us a
happy comfortable end.
Some of us are afraid of it.
It makes us worry about events we can't see yet
Or that have already passed away.
The past is the most visited interval of time
amongst the majority of people.
We go there in school.
We go there with family,
Reminiscing on the good old days.
Sometimes we look so far into the past that we birth
old pains anew in our lives.
We conjure up things that have long since passed
And we hurt ourselves trying to destroy or rekindle
things that were lost.
Sometimes we bring the pain of yesterday with us
into today which leaves a lasting mark on our
throats.
The only problem is that it has our handprint written
all over it.
Surprisingly enough the hand of the future happens
to have a similar effect

Except this either leads us into action
Or causes us to stagger in our lifelong pursuit of
worth.
The future has a way of making us second guess
ourselves.
It makes us anxious
Nervous
Sometimes it leaves us scattered in our minds
There's no telling what it holds
We can see glimpses of what it may seem to have
in store,
But to our minds, doing that is on par with chores.
We can't control time because it never changes its
pattern though we worry about it exclusively
When we can mold our present day to
Build the foundation for tomorrow
It's the simple things we overcomplicate.
A problem as easy as 2+2 could be changed
dramatically if a stray X just so happened to get
involved without explanation,
Then the rest of the alphabet decides to join the
party and solving the equation is now
A problem because the room left on the board is
unimaginably large...
Although there's an equation/ formula /reason for
all of our lives.
We can not bow down to uncertainty and lose sight
of the original equation.
It always starts simple until we add the alphabet.
The alphabet filled with unnecessary worrying and
anxiety
Taking priority

Of the sole majority of our brain's space.
The space we need to breathe is constantly
occupied by arbitrary things.
Step back and breathe, a therapist will tell you.
Center your mind, a meditation coach will tell you.
Breathe in, breathe out, a yoga instructor will tell
you.
Let it go, a friend will tell you.
I can't, you tell yourself.
Some things are harder to let pass than others
Trauma is unforgettable
But something simple is like an irritating pimple.
You want it gone but you have to put action
Into getting rid of it.
At the end of the day, we all have a choice,
We swim out of the water and breathe,
Or we reach out and ask for help.
We're too weak alone to live a life where we cannot
breathe,
That is why venting is called venting
Because it is the act of relieving stress
Off of one's chest
Or a release of something,
A discharge.
We've got to enlarge our breathing space
And diminish the walls of
Anguish
And it's many additions to nothing but hurdles.
We have to breathe and so does this world.

~THE WORLD'S WALK~

The way this world spins is crazy
Sometimes what happens is that we get lazy

Things have been changing a lot lately.
A lot of things are escalating
But most are dark and often hazy,
Like a crime scene
After someone goes missing.
Our world is limping.
Left, skip, right, like it's pimping.
Its life in this universe is beyond lengthy
And we've been here technically
For seconds really.
We each have legs,
Some stand on pegs,
Or other mechs.
We walk,
Stride,
Ride
The road of life
This world can only rotate as long as the
gravitational pull around it in space holds up.
Why does it seem like it's stopped?
Like someone stuck their fingers in the clock
Causing time and space to halt
What are we hiding in the vault
That will lead to our advancement as people?
If you read a book in a series
There is most definitely a sequel
Or a rewrite.
The first stripe is the next generation
The future of the nations
Of this world.
Some may give it a whirl but others would rather
squirrel through life

And hide
When the bitter winds attack.
That's ok
Because the world walks
but spins.
If we want to keep moving
We have to step forward.
Backward is not cutting it anymore.
It is imperative that
We stop repeating the past
Reverse effects exist
And so many of us are living them right now
through
Racism,
sexism(man vs woman),
Religious persecution.
Well that's a shortlist but it's passed
Further and further
Down the line of generations
From you to yours
From theirs to theirs
From then to now
From the past came a lot of things
But a lot haunts the structure of society
With a dehumanizing presence.
Guinea pig mentality spreads today like a
Virus in the air.
You can say that's not fair
But I hope you're aware that
What you know and how you act
Is in high regard of how you were taught
School can't teach you how to act or treat people

People do.
That's why as little kids we haunt our parents
Watching their every move
Taking in intel.
Because parents are the ones we watch to
determine our mode of action.
They're supposed to be the mature ones of the
bunch.
Keyword is <u>Supposed</u>
The thing is that not everyone is going to be that
way
And society is the same likewise.
The perfect people
Are not perfect
And the broken people are not always broken.
Sometimes the eye is deceiving.
It sees only on the external frontier
But rarely the internal affairs.
Have you ever watched someone with a limp walk?
They focus their weight on one leg or foot,
Simply favoring the strength of one over the other.
Why do they do this?
Well because simply one leg/foot can not support
the weight it should regularly hold.
This is like our lifestyles
We limp on the side that <u>physically</u> shows "who we
are"
The tangible side if you will,
This is the extension of our clothes, and
accessories, the way we talk and walk, how we
take care of ourselves.

Some of this will give hints of the side that is rarely revealed,
The one that's lightly tapped on the ground before it's quickly withdrawn.
Who we are on the inside.
It's easy to act with a mask on,
Dancing on the outside while you stagger helplessly on the inside.
Anyone happy on the outside can be dying on the inside,
Anyone sad on the outside can be joyous as all outdoors on the inside, that's just how they look.
the inverse respect is true but the reflective respect is true also.
How can you tell if what is portrayed is real or not?
How can you tell if someone is true to who they really are or not?
What are we hiding that causes us to trip up?
It's not always easy to decipher a painting's meaning or true intended message.
It is often not as direct or simple as it may seem.
Everything has an underlying message,
A hidden core to its piece,
A focal point that doesn't quite catch the eye of the beholder until it is revealed by the artist.
We can paint ourselves in an image easily
And cover up exactly what we want to cover until someone asks.
Questions often catch people off guard
Because for some reason in today's society
No one asks how others are doing unless someone will do it for them.

One-sided affairs are often what we catch
ourselves stuck in,
The artist knows everything and doesn't have to
reveal a thing.
We don't apply care to our conversations as much
as friends should.
Most of our conversations revolve around gossip
and anything unrelated to the beautiful work of art
in front of us.
How often do we study each other?
A lot of people will shift pertaining to a specific
environment.
Sometimes it's related to the requirement
And other times it relates to who one truly is when
either they aren't trying to impress someone or hide
something.
If we'd ask questions we'd learn the reason for said
limp.
People don't wear visible boots in their heads.
You can't see what they fight inside unless they
show you or tell you truthfully in that matter.
It's not easy to interpret a trained limp.
What does trained limp mean?
It means they've played a role for so long that it's
become like a part of their nature.
Nature, like the instinctive way to act in a given
situation.
They become the bootleg version of themselves.
Few people in this world can tell when someone is
not themself.
Parents have this ability because they knew their
child before they even spoke,

They watch carefully.
Children aren't the only ones learning in these situations.
Adults, no matter how mature, have to learn as well.
Some older people don't even know themselves.
You ever wonder why a midlife crisis occurs?
I do it all the time.
Maybe it happens because routine sucks.
Maybe it happens because they're bored.
Or maybe it happens because they lose sight of themselves in the preluding events.
The way someone walks tells a lot about them.
Their level of confidence,
Comfortability,
Relational status,
Status in general,
Interests,
Goals,
Etc etc.
The look in one's eye as they walk tells you their intention.
In the walk of life, a lot of people realize that we're on a pothole-filled road.
We have to stride carefully to not sink.
Sometimes we trip but that's why we must stand again.
A lot of us fall once and consider ourselves a failure,
No one is ever a failure until they lay on the ground and give up for good.

How many of us have fallen and haven't felt like getting up?
I know I have and the first word on my mind was fudge!
Thinking about fudge, it reminds me of a chocolate fountain,
It never stops letting that glorious plume of chocolate spurt out of its top.
The only way to stop it is if you pull the plug.
The beauty of it makes you want to stare at it for hours.
That's like us, we're beautiful until we pull the plug on ourselves.
We stop our flow without ever stopping to see it for ourselves
We start to dry up and meld
With the concrete placed before us as challenges to teach us how to move.
Hardship is present in everyone's life
But giving up should never be an option
There is hope in even the darkest places.
If there's a dark tunnel there's sure to be an exit to the light and a path to get you there.
Nothing is ever hidden forever.
A truth and a lie will be revealed the same in the end.
Walking straight and being true to who you are will serve much more beneficial than
Swaying left and right trying to fit the exterior mantra of the ideal societal person.
Be authentically you to a fault
Don't be tricked by who you think you are

Be who you know you are.
You'll end up walking listlessly in a forest of misinterpretation if you wander to a place you know you don't belong unless you're led by the right principle.
Life targets no one.
It does its job perfectly.
You can't fight life and it won't wrestle with you.
Your choices affect those around you as much as they affect you.
Think about that as you stop limping and start walking the right way.
Straight up and confident.

~THE TALK OF THIS WORLD~

Walk the walk.
Talk the talk.
There's a lot of talk
Floating around in the air but not a lot of action
It's a lot like gossip.
We have opinions but no reaction
We live in an unorthodox fashion
What realm do we cash in?
Where are we joining the movement of positive action
Moving with genuine passion
These things shouldn't be left for ration
Not in this or the next nation.
The news will tell you what's going on
But they won't move away from the mic.
Instagram can show or tell you an issue but
It won't help.
Sometimes words without action hold no weight.

So what are we going to talk about that we'll change?
Gossip is only good for conversation
And even that is foolhardy.
What does one get from that?
Kicks and giggles maybe.
But after the fact what are we going to do with it?
We can't do anything with words alone,
There is a limited amount of substance in a conversation that doesn't last or have a true effect.
It doesn't make sense for people to say something and not move unless they are afraid.
Be a man/woman of your word.
If you say you're going to do something
And you don't do it
Shame on you.
Now, if you say you're going to do something stupid and don't do it, then you may be wise
Or just stupid with a conscious.
What intention do our words hold?
Do we believe in what we say?
We say a lot of pointless things that amount to nothing but empty conversation.
I'm not saying we have to live by everything we say
But we'd better be cautious as to what context we say things in.
There's a thing about words that holds a weight incomparable to sticks and stones
There is a poem written in "*Confessions Poetry Collection Volume* 2" by Emmanuel Wallace.
 that goes like this,
"Sticks and stones may break my bones

But words, words will forever haunt me if I let them.
I am the plant and they become the stem
Like ghosts, they push and push me into sin
Words, words...they haunt me
Echoing in and out of my head
How many tears will I shed?
GOD
There's a drought,
Within I'm without
Words
I. I can't see the end but
Here they come again
They haunt me.
One slithers in
Then comes the next
I am perplexed.
They strip away my best
I'm stuck in my funeral vest
I'm not blessed.
Sticks and stones may break my bones
But words, words will forever haunt me,
Words
They don't even attack from the outside
But they charge at my heart from the inside
Why haven't I died?
How many times has my mind lied,
Whispering deathly words into my open blinds
I can't deny
I can resign
I can't be left blind
My heart is my biggest enemy and my greatest ally
But when these hellish words hit my mind

I wonder why
Why do they stick longer than words of life?
The ones that'll take me high
Right now, I crave to shine
But these words pollute my mind
Sticks and stones may break my bones but words,
words will forever haunt me if I let them.
Word."
If you listen to these words simply as you read
them
You'd understand that words are not always gentle
and they are the ones that take action in a lot of
cases.
Our voices hold weight but we can only see a
surface-level reaction.
Just like in this world when we say things and
We can only see the effect they have on others and
their lives on a surface level.
Talk is cheap they say,
Action is expensive.
Not a lot of us are willing to move.
I'm talking on statements
Fueled by good intention,
Passion for growth and development,
Dreams, and choice.
We're so stagnant in ourselves
That we forget that there is much more available if
only we moved on what we feel called to do
pertaining to advancement and purpose.
So much is lost because few are willing to move
with what they feel led to do.

Have you ever heard someone express their desire
and watch them do anything but what it is they said
they declared?
There are quite a few instances of fear-based
stagnation.
Change is different
And different requires change.
Walk the walk
talk the talk
It's a simple concept
Each line requires the other
Whence do we speak
And when will we move?
Our words must be fueled by the action of our feet.
In the spirit of talking
What is our conversation about?
Who are we talking about?
Why are we talking about them?
Why are we so focused on everything but what we
can improve?
Now we're talking about literal talking
Why are we so focused on dragging other
Down into the dirt before us?
Why does it seem like failure is more prominent in
conversation to belittle success?
Why do we feed off of the gossip that I've been
stressing continually that doesn't lead to anything.
Gossip is a waste of time.
It's a way to turn the attention that we need to have
put on developing ourselves to pinpointing minor
inconveniences in anyone other than the one who
needs help.

What is gossip?
Gossip is idle talk or rumor, especially about the personal or private affairs of others.
Keyword
Idle
This means without purpose or effect,
In other words, pointless.
It would make sense to let it go,
Except for the fact that there will always be something we want that others have.
And the only way we can get it is by imagining we were better than them.
Envy is a childish gamble.
You want something?
Work for it.
Complaining is going to do nothing but leave you bottled up in a jar of despair.
We catch ourselves looking left to right
Claiming "I want that"
"One day that'll be mine."
But what are we doing to do such things?
And why are we basing our future on what
Other people have?
We all have a voice
But few of us choose to use it.
We all have potential
But most of us set it off to the sideline and pursue money.
Money rules our lives and our conversation.
If someone has it,
We're talking about it.
If someone doesn't have it

We're talking about it.
We try to use the concept of money and our word
phrases to cause wars,
To gain power over those who earned their wealth.
We try to use our words to distort
Societal proportions
And to dictate other people's lives.
We can't walk because we are tying our legs
around people who are already struggling to stay
upright.
So many of us act as leeches that
We use people
And manipulate their hearts.
Our words if we don't check them sting like darts
And act as nails to our own feet,
Pinning us in perfect stagnation.
It's like creating an excuse for procrastination.
We can't walk because we're too busy talking.
My saying is "if you're going to talk (especially trash
talk) you'd better make sure you can back it up."
There's another issue right there
Not a lot of us are working with evidence as our
backup.
We rely on assumption
And consumption.
That's why rich people don't dress the stereotypical
way,
And people who want, do exactly that.
We live in a world of appearances fixated on the
Surface level.
We never stop to study
And we never stop to listen.

It seems like we're so caught up in ourselves that
We can not physically open our eyes and ears to
our surroundings.
Well, I guess that's a dead art because people start
to feel some type of way when you remain silent
while they talk.
Sometimes adding more fuel to an already raging
fire is pointless.
If you feed people what they want they'll want
more.
Like a dog that returns to its puke, we keep on
returning to the darkness for more.
It surprises me how easily grand things are spoken,
How words of death and life are easily spread
across the nationsas tokens
But action is rare.
This is a comparison filled world
Where if I don't have what you have,
I'm not good enough.
If you aren't like me,
Don't even bother trying to make my acquaintance.
If I am different,
Being an outcast is normal.
If I look
Talk
Walk
Think even in a slightly different manner
I am not worthy of your time.
Our world is stereotypical
Why is it that an educated black kid is called white?
Why is it that clothes automatically determine rich
or poor?

Why is it that kids are deemed immature when secretly they know more than they let off?
Why is it that in schools kids can't breathe yet we call it a safe environment?
We're conditioned as youth to walk and talk in the way of a worker.
We are not inspired enough to make choices that are outside of the curriculum.
Choices that with action and voice could change our whole perspective on life.
Why is it that life is considered a curse worse than death?
Can we not see that we have been gifted with so many things that are stifled by opinion?
Who are we trying to please?
It's like we're trying to look at everyone else's reflective view of ourselves before checking for ourselves.
We love to solve everyone else's mysteries but when it comes to our own we're clueless.
Do I know myself?
Have you asked yourself this recently?
Probably not
It's not uncommon for us to talk big one day and go home and contemplate how impossible it is.
I think that instead of focusing on what's impossible We should look at the ways to make it possible.
Maybe that way we'd forget about trying to copy everyone else and find our own route with the help that some (not all) people can offer.
People will not believe in you right away
But they will watch.

You have their attention.
When you move you become more visible and
People can see you because the further and further
away you get from their frozen grasp,
The more and more they want to follow you.
We have a hard time seeing others succeed ahead
of us.
That's a part of our supposed competitive nature.
The special thing about moving is that you never
have to look back at who's trying to drag you back
Because they are the ones who will have to move
forward to get a hold of you.
Walk the walk
Talk the talk
Only one works when the other is present.

~THE WORLD'S CRY~

Hear me this day for I have raised my voice to
behold you.
Lend me your ear for the time is near.
Either move or run away,
The time is near.
An uprising of change shall wash my face
And all will see,
But it'll only last a moment,
A momentary chance for you to move
For more,
I cannot see but I can feel
My speed has dwindled and my hope has faded,
Where are you oh man
That you can mend the broken bonds amongst the
species?
You are man and I am a geostructure,

You are responsible
As much as I.
The product of your expedition whether it be
beneficial or detrimental
Is my responsibility to produce.
How I look is a reflection of your works,
Either you spoil or cleanse me;
But for a majority, I am spoiled rotten
With junk,
Disgusting feces,
Waste, and
That's how you treat me.
That's how you greet me.
Hear my cry because I hear yours!
You ignore me
Yet I adhere to your command.
You may have dominion
But you act like a minion to everyone around you.
How hard is it to live for more than yourselves?
We talk about realms,
Ranges,
Places And spaces,
Love,
Hate,
Conversation,
Each nation
Split by its own vocation
That's the notification we need to look at.
That was the world speaking.
This is not the world speaking now,
This is another human
Speaking to more humans

If we heard our friend say these same things in the
context of a human,
If your best friend were to say ,
Hear me today because I have sought you
YOU
I sought you out
Listen to me because my time is near
You can either help me or leave me behind
My time is near
change has to occur that I might survive
Our relationship will die unless we both change
Even if it only lasts for a moment,
There is a major chance for us to succeed
I can't see it
But I can feel it.
Our growth has dwindled
And I can't sense any growth within myself.
You can only see what I show you
But I'm dying inside,
I feel alone even when I tell you
I need help.
We're different
But that makes sense... Although we have things in
common, I need your help.
I'm hurting.
What would you say?
What would you do?
I'm not saying stop eating meat
And I'm not saying give up everything
What I'm saying is that we need to be more
Perceptive of the things that occur around us
And if we are,

We need to bring it to terms we can understand.
Friends should be of importance to us
Or have some kind of value,
Some kind of substance in our lives .
Some kind of worth.
What's different with the world?
I mean we live with it every day
We live with ourselves every day
If our friend were dying we'd lend a hand
When our world is dying we turn bland.
Is there a care to give?
I can't answer for you,
That liberty is your own.
When the word cry is uttered
Immediately tears,
Sobbing
Brokenness floods the mind's eye.
But in this case, it's an indirect direct call to action.
Hear my cry!
Hear my call!
He cried out
He spoke in a loud voice.
Different context, different results.
Hear the world's cry,
You see me, do you see my wounds
All of those times I risked my life for you
I never feared what lies behind the tomb
Because I dedicated my all to you.
I bet you wish I was through
But no I have something great to protect too
I'll put my blood, sweat, and tears
Into it until I feel them rushing out of my ears

I can't allow that presence of fear.
You see me, do you see my wounds
It's been this way from the womb
I was born to protect
Ever since we met
I chose you.
I'd lay my life down like an all In bet
I won't die knowing you're upset.
For years I watched the stars
As they climbed further and further away like this
time of ours.
I'll bear these scars forever
They all make me better
All of the cuts and tears I took for you
I wouldn't even regard them as wounds
But it makes sense right?
You've watched me jump in front of fire for you
Walk the thin wire for you
That's because you're a part of me too.
I am the past and you are the present
The future is determined by your acceptance
I battled so you can relax
I lost so you could win
I cried so you could smile
Do you understand that I am about to pass?
Look at me one more time as the last.
You will forever wield my scars,
But they will be the reason you shine like the
morning star
Because you embraced them and let the pain go
So they could be like priceless etching on aged
stone.

You will never be perfect
But you can be whole
Regardless of my battles, I welcome you home
To the present go back
And be like me
Fight for a better future and then you'll see
My wounds
My scars
Just me.
We do not worship the world but we must move to
protect it.
We are responsible.

~DANCE~

move rhythmically to music, typically following a set
sequence of steps.
a new form of communication
We talk,
We sign,
We feel,
But have you ever seen anyone communicate
Through dance?
Look at the trees in the storms.
Look at the clouds in the morning.
Look at the waves
How they sway left and right,
Forwards and back.
Watch how the leaves swish with the wind
And how the grass mimics the water.
Dance attracts
And frightens
The same.
It's used to seduce and hypnotize an audience

Or arouse it the same.
Dance is an eruption of physical motion that
Captures the eye
But projects the soul.
This is genuine dancing,
Not twerking
And all of that jazz
But dancing to portray a message bigger than what
the eye can see.
It touches the soul.
Do you ever wonder if your soul dances?
Or your heart when it's filled with joy?
It's hard to pacify true emotion.
Passion is the root of natural intent
Featured on the soul's palette.
The same is to be said about words in a book,
They swim through your mind
As you try to decide
What they're supposed to mean.
Sometimes something complex could mean the
simplest thing.
Sometimes the simple can easily be translated into
something excruciatingly complex.
But when one dances
It doesn't matter.
The way they move correlates with the music,
The tone set before them.
Every movement is controlled by the heart.
Sometimes choreography only goes so far.
It's up to the dancer's interpretation
It's not the dance that defines the dancer
But the connection they have to the music that

Influences their body to move accordingly.
Moving,
Action,
According to a tone set externally
That connects with what lies in wait dormant
Inside of us.
We are all our own dancers.
How we move is according to the tone that is set for us by life.
It's a pain how we only have a small say in the hand life deals us.
It's hard to know that where we're born,
How we're born
Isn't in our hands.
But how we live after we're born
Is completely our choice,
The tone and rhythm of the song we're dealt to play with
Is completely in our hands after it starts.
How it touches our hearts is completely in our control.
Every moment in life has a role .
Just as every shoe has a sole.
There are sticks and stones on every road
But that's all they are,
We can trip but we can always right ourselves
And keep dancing.
The tragedy of life is that sometimes other people will toss such obstacles in front of you because they want you to stumble.
Life will throw them in to show you how to step
And reform your dance.

Your flow should only change when your dance is fixing to grow more elegant.
Surety is what life offers with its obstacles.
It wishes to show us that as we step we must
Be able to be free with our movements.
You know, when you watch a dancer,
The spotlight follows them around because as they move their freedom draws the light towards them.
We have to realize that if we run away from life's challenges
And adhere to the obstacles men and women will place in our paths,
We are sure to fall and break our ankles in the dark.
Blood, sweat, and passionate tears
Flow with the metronome of life,
No one is exempt in this world.
Pain comes to even the best dancers,
But they are willing to sacrifice
So that they can improve.
Our toes may be stubbed at first but soon they'll be clean.
Our legs and body may be sore at first but soon they'll be strong.
Our hearts may be uncertain at first but soon they will be sure.
Everyone's dance is unique to them
But the beauty within is to be shared the same.
We cannot be defeated by our own hand,
But we like to give it all the power.
Like I said earlier, we suffocate ourselves.
Drugs are not the way

Recreational sex is not the way
Partying is not the way
Fighting is not the way
Acceptance is not the way.
Just dance, let it flow and you'll find that the
Freedom and peace you need is inside of you,
Your faith,
The love you receive and give,
Your heart.
There is power in releasing yourself from the blame
Game.
Life is not to blame.
No one is to blame in this life but ourselves when
we don't get to where we wish to.
God puts things in our way to elevate us,
People in our way to educate us,
Places in our path to introduce us,
Checkpoints to mark.
All of these are to help us elevate our dance
So people can see us.
Sometimes walking gets boring
It feels pointless sometimes
Everyone that can walk walks physically
But not everyone that can dance dances.
Some of us wait until we're excited to dance.
Some of us can't because we're stuck to the
ground by expectation.
Our feet hurt worse when we stand still.
Imagine lifting your feet nimbly off of the ground
Waltzing in the wind like a leaf in the morning sway
Swishing left and right like the like the waves of the
sea,

Back and forth like the rustling trees,
Imagine dancing like a wrongly convicted felon
finally released from a prison in which he did not
belong.
Imagine a bird stretching its wings.
Imagine a wolf let out of a reserve into its natural
habitat.
What if we were living in our element?
Free.
Because I know some of us although we're trying to
dance.
Feel like on our ankles there's a ball and chain
Holding us down from our true and glorious
potential.
Have you ever realized how refreshing it is to let go
of sin?
Sure it's a biblical term but it best sums up the dark
along with the works of the flesh which are painfully
shallow.
They can be found in Galatians 5:19-21 in the Bible
If you read through that twice you'll see what I
mean.
Emptiness comes when you walk after temporary
things.
Imagine a dancer stopping mid-dance, falling, and
staying down for the rest of the count.
That'd be disappointing to see if you cared.
Why would a dancer trip themselves intentionally?
That's what it's like chasing shallow concepts and
things.
But guess what comes right after those two verses,

The 9 greatest dance moves for any dancer
(person) to inherit.
The fruit of the spirit.
Love
Joy
Peace
Longsuffering
Gentleness
Goodness
Faith
Meekness
Temperance
You can find those in Galatians 5:22.
The words that make them so different is works and
fruit.
You can not consume works but works can
consume you.
Fruit can only nourish you and your body and it's
free for you to consume if you so choose to grow it.
The more effort you put into trying to be like and
have what the next man has, the less unique and
pure your dance becomes.
We must focus on ourselves so that we may supply
others with hope.
The problem with today's society is that self-care is
deemed as forgetting about everyone and doing
everything to boost our own egos.
Sometimes we just need to dance alone so that we
can understand our own dance.
One day someone will raise the question,
Why do you move like that?

How would you respond if you didn't know for
yourself?
The one thing you would notice when you
reevaluate your dance is that the fuel behind it is
Either for you to grow
Or against you to be accepted.
The two relate to the works of the flesh and the fruit
of the spirit.
Ladies and gentlemen
The object of dance is to be completely authentic
To the essence of our souls.
If we cannot walk then we shall dance .
Move in such a way it draws attention because it
won't be your body shining but your soul shining
through you.
This world needs more dancers
But if you knew where I meant for the dance to
occur (your heart) then you have the key to free
form movement.

THE DROUGHT OF THE WORLD

A land deprived of substance cannot bring forth
substance.
What does this mean?
If a flower has no water can it grow?
No, but can a seed without soil grow?
No,
A land deprived of substance can be best
represented as a desert.
Barren and
Sand laden.
Water is scarce
And civilization is rare.

But even in a desert one can find an oasis.
Sandstorms refuse to cover them up
Why?
Substance.
It appears nature loves to preserve that which
provides it nutrients.
An oasis is described amongst travelers as the
saving grace of the unknown.
No one once they're in the grasp of the desert
Knows when their journey will end until it ends.
Say you were a traveler in a barren land,
How long would you last until you crumbled to your
knees?
How long would it be for you to beg God for water?
How long would it be before you gave in to the
brutal atmosphere of those desolate lands?
In this world we are barren
A lot of people are wasting away in hate.
Our oasis is care/love.
A shallow pool of water runs out quickly,
It'll dry out swiftly under the brutal sun of society.
Our lives are run by the hands of its clock.
We run according to how people order us
We walk to where people toss us.
How many of us are crawling around in a bare
world?
Some of us are trying to seek refuge in the lands of
people who eat away at substance without
hesitation.
Like leeches drinking your life away.
Water is a precious resource that we all need to
live,

Much like love.
But people are abused
And used for the love they give.
People lose their desire to love others because
People these days can't accept it and send some back.
Instead, they feed off of it until there's none left to receive,
And there's none left to give.
We suck the substance out of each other until there is none left.
Eventually, if we refuse to value the small oasis that some people give others access to drink,
There will be no more.
Imagine sitting beside an oasis and as you drink you begin to take in sand.
You try to fill your flask
And you attempt to drink.
What do you get?
Sand.
Would you want to drink sand?
I wouldn't.
What do we offer others that they may
Retain substance?
Every now and then even the most abundant bodies of water need to be resupplied.
If we take take take
And it never rains
What do you think will happen?
There will be nothing left but salt and sand.
I'm talking about relationships again.
If we drink and drink and drink

Do we really think we'll win?
If anything we'll get heavy and lose
Something more valuable than the water itself.
The source.
When we separate from love we introduce
ourselves to an internal divorce.
We can take and take
But in reality, it will not fill our own oasis until we
reciprocate.
Selfish waters eventually overflow and lose most of
their substance, destroying countless lands in its
wake.
We are in such a drought around this world
because people who genuinely care and will give
freely,
are dried out.
So many people like this give up
They give up because they feel as if they don't
matter.
Like their substance was for naught.
Giving seems weak
Because it's weakening after a while.
The strongest people will give more from their
hearts than their pockets.
Love can not be paid for by money,
Because then it loses its real value.
Therefore it is taken as a grain of salt
Let alone a grain of sand in the eyes of the supplier.
How hard is it to care for one another?
I know it's best not to look for anything in return
But sometimes after a while

Emptiness is dreadful, especially if what's given is abused.
It is more rewarding when the substance given is utilized wisely and taken seriously.
It is more rewarding to see someone spread the substance than to receive it back sometimes.
The return is its beneficial usage.
An oasis isn't water to be thrown out into the scorching sand.
What is the purpose if we waste it?
So much is wasted in this life.
In this world
Yet we can not see it unless it happens to us.
Sometimes words hold little significance.
They often fall on deaf ears.
Revenge is not a necessity
It isn't worth the time,
Energy or effort.
If a dry place could dig just a little deeper there is water to be found.
Even in the earth's crust, this is to be true.
We must dig wells within ourselves so that we never run out of substance to give.
And so that we have room to receive it,
Retain it,
Utilize it beneficially,
And value it.
When we have to dig a little deeper things seem to be worth a lot more.
We can supply and nourish others just as much as ourselves.

God can refill the wells of our spirits if we'd open up
to his love and kindness.
Divine love exists but even that,
We take for granted,
Granted if we understood why it existed.
Love exists to free us from dry emptiness.
Yet our world is at its lowest.
Quality substance is running out
But we all have room for more.
It makes little sense to me how we can receive love
and then never give it to someone else.
Life is much more than what we can get.
If we're always focusing on what we can receive
Eventually, all we'll be digesting is sand.
The word drought means
a prolonged period of abnormally low rainfall,
leading to a shortage of water.
Or a prolonged absence of something specified.
We're missing something important
It's about time we stopped stripping it away and
started giving/receiving it openly.
What I am speaking of is not sexual
It is beyond that, it is spiritual and substantial.
We've got to escape this ongoing drought of
Empty substance.

~SOCIAL WORLD~

We are social beings.
We are not strong alone.
So we try making ways to connect,
Technology for example.

When we talk about technology in today's terms,
the first idea that pops into our heads is robots, but
we don't all have access to those.
The number one thing that everyone *does* have in
their household,
pocket,
bookbag,
or purse is a phone.
A phone is this small electric box we hold in our
hands for hours upon hours at a time.
When phones were first created, they were tailored
to connect us all as people and help us find
common ground from miles away.
This was the new way to communicate when you
weren't close enough to talk in person.
 It worked out great back in that time.
Things have changed drastically.
These days we are easily exposed to the illusion of
connectivity.
We can see people.
We can watch what they're doing daily.
We can do this on Instagram,
Snapchat,
Facebook,
and a host of other streaming and social media
platforms but
We see so many particles of people living their
"best life,"
but in reality, they are only snippets of the best
moments.
We become followers.

More of us in this day and age become followers more than we are friends.
We live for the curtain called fame.
This fictional reality has become our new habitat.
We live in the snippets of other people's lives,
and we learn envy.
We desire to be like them, especially as younger people, because we want what *they* have.
We want *their* fame,
Their money,
Their girls,
Their boys,
Their families even;
We just want to look the part.
How can we say we are connected when we shove ourselves into a false reality?
losing ourselves trying to create a realistic illusion of prosperity.
The connectivity I'm talking about today is not the interaction between us as a group, but the interaction we have with ourselves.
This is new technology.
With so many fantasies created by the social eye, many struggles appear especially when we try to grasp who *we* are.
Some of us would go broke to look like we have it made.
Some of us cry at night because although we got 50k likes on a post, something is still missing.
Some of us sit in silence, staring at a wall, wondering,
guessing who our *real friends are.*

Some of us just live life feeling like outcasts because we don't have the required amount of followers to feel valid.

We don't meet the curriculum.

Isolation begins when one feels as if they don't exist in a specified realm.

Isolation is when one feels like a ghost amongst men.

The Iso Effect is when one gets so attached to an ideal thing that they forget who they are.

The Iso Effect impacts a lot of stuff, which is where people's connectivity comes into play.

People interact in several ways.

We talk,

text,

or call,

our three primary choices of communication.

With technology specifically,

This can become a problem.

Shy people, although they now have an easy platform to communicate,

will resort to texting instead of talking,

and they begin to become dependant on responses.

More often than not, they may never get one unless they know that person(s) directly.

The feeling of rejection is more potent because

They know that the person they texted has a phone,

and they know that person has a minute to look at their DMs.

That rejection and extra knowledge fuels the feeling
of insignificance.
The same thing occurs with posts or stories.
Suppose we don't get "X" amount of likes,
shares,
Or views something is wrong with us.
With so many gateways present at our fingertips,
it's beyond easy to lose touch.
Sometimes we begin to hate people we don't even
know
because our desire to have the same luxury is
robust.
Sometimes we become so jealous
or bitter at ourselves that we take it out on others.
We live in the "land of all great conversations,"
The comments.
The trouble people go through to control and
manipulate someone's life through social media
because of a snippet is otherworldly.
 How can we be connected when division flashes
us in our faces as we scroll through our feed?
We carry out arguments and battles in the media.
And since it has so much influence,
more and more people see this and make
judgments against one another, targeting the
opposing group.
We target each other so we can feel like a part of a
group.
This social division is not healthy.
To top it off from a more direct standpoint, when we
can talk to anyone at any given time over text, it
becomes hard to communicate in person.

The experience goes both ways;
if you speak to someone religiously over text and
barely in person, it is beyond awkward when you
meet up.
You don't know their interpersonal personality
because over text, you have time to think and plan.
Real conversation matters, and
if we can't do that because we prefer to hide,
it becomes hard to connect on an absolute level.
This all goes to say that although technology and
the media have their benefits, the glaring issue is
that people are stretching further and further apart.
The only solution to this issue is to take a step
away from these things and find yourself.
Take a break from the media's uncontrollable
current and take time to understand your current
situation because
I believe that when we truly understand ourselves,
we can genuinely connect with others.
That is the only way we can divert the Iso Effect.
That's the only way we can have a truly social world
When we stop judging,
Comparing,
And ravening over snippets.
We cannot be social if we are divided.
This raises the question of social media
Is it social or just...

~THE WORLD'S MEDIA~

Is corrupt
It leaves us stuck in a sea
Of false reality
Contingency,

And ending scenes
That don't exist.
This world's media is focused on what?
The demise Or rise of others.
Media,
A.K.A the main means of mass communication.
How are we using it?
To communicate the darkness,
What I mean when I say this
Is that we communicate what we reflect.
So the media dives into the darkness of the world
and elevates it.
Because what?
Because the world around us is increasingly dark
and it seems to be the acceptable route.
So why not give it the exposure it can thrive upon?
If you feed the fire
You can't expect it to shrink.
Social media today is focused on three things
The rich, the famous, and the broken.
Then there are subsidiary units known as the
Sexy, eye-catching, flesh pleasers.
It's all you hear about these days.
We try so hard to live in everyone else's lives,
Everyone else's drawls,
Everyone else's experiences,
That we end up dragging them into a rut with our
expectations.
They're so exposed that our expectation rules their
lives.
This is what I was talking about in the world's fame.

People can't live when the media is so focused on
their downfall;
But downfall isn't the correct word for this instance
The correct word would be tea
Which is better known as gossip.
What does gossip do for anybody
Besides entertain one's ego?
Nothing.
And we wonder why celebrities keep their
monumental moments private.
We wonder why people are afraid to be
themselves.
We wonder why things are not changing in this
world.
Because WHAT ARE WE HIGHLIGHTING?
I don't see a lot of pure content,
Instead, I see booty and money,
And I don't follow those types of pages.
You look on apps like tik tok
The challenges that do the best are the ones where
someone is shaking their butt in some way.
The media highlights anything that would be
pleasing to the eye.
In other instances, we love to,
As the media,
Highlight the failure of others.
Although failure is the root of success
Everyone these days is afraid of humiliation
It's not even the fact that they'll fail
It's the fact that everyone around them,
If they're big enough will eat away at them if they
mess up.

No man is safe when the world is watching.
The youth of this world are subject to the idea of
perfection or death.
There is no in-between
This is why kids struggle to express themselves
Because the environment they are in appears
judgemental,
And no one is setting a healthy example around
them.
The media doesn't help because it claws at
insecurities,
Showing the "perfect" job
"Perfect" body
"Perfect" life
And who do you think is watching that closely and
comparing that to where they are today?
The youth.
Motivational speakers these days spend more time
yelling and cursing that their message loses its
credibility.
How're you going to help someone using words
that don't penetrate the soul?
Curse words are empty words filling imaginary
spaces.
Kids adopt that language because it seems like an
acceptable dialect.
The youth of this world are dying,
Their originality is suffering
Trends rule the world
And they're ruling our lives.
The media portrays the darkness.
How often is the light brought to the spotlight

Unless it's dug up from the dirt above it?
Rarely.
This is the world we live in
We're feeding the fire of emptiness
We gossip about the people who worked to get to
where they are
We hate the things that expose the darkness and
offer an opportunity for the light.
It's different.
You can't mold the truth.
Therefore we resort to hiding it,
Burying it until someone notices.
Not enough people care though.
Our own skin is what matters 24/7
We compare ourselves and we gossip to feel good
about our current position.
We expose the darkness because it's easy to
accept.
We leave the light in the shadows because it's too
"controversial"
People are dying
Yet we're focused on trends.
Kids are dying to conformity.
Yet we're focused on what the next man has.
The world is ending.
Yet we're focused on what pleases us in the
moment.
Our role models are disappearing
Yet it does not matter.
The idea of respect is fading
Yet we don't care.
Hope is at a fatal loss

But everyone claims they pray.
We are what we eat,
When one says you are what you eat we often
assume it is the food placed on the table but it is
not.
It is the people we spend time around,
the videos we choose to watch,
the music we listen to, etc.
We digest these things every day. So, we need to
be careful of what we choose to savor.
The media and us have no idea what we're feeding
And putting into this reality.
It's a beast that can only be tamed by the light.
The problem is,
The light is fading because it is wielded mainly by
the youth,
Who have the most access to the media.
There isn't enough urgency when it comes to
encouraging the light
Because according to the media there is only one
way to go to achieve one's true potential.
Everything is so sporadic that decisions become
easy,
Death over life.
Darkness over light.
Chase and never seek.
Run but never wait.
Move but never learn.
Claim but never study.
Talk but never listen.
Fight but never peace.
Bound but never free.

This is what the chaos of the media is;
The chaos of what we feed ourselves is.
Our world will be broken if we do not change what
we pour our focus into.
Love is not hard if we understand that not
everything is a battle.
Peace would be easy if we would lose our pride.
This is life though.
Few take heed and others gobble it up and spit it
out onto the pavement.
The issue is,
 that pavement is the foothold of death.
Our world is dead on the inside
as are a multitude of people resting on its face.
Watch what you put on your plate because you
never know how it'll digest in the end.
Our differences are what make us unique
But there are right and wrong,
Unnecessary and arbitrary,
Some of us have to understand that it's not that
hard to admit fault.
This is the world and the media controls it.

~THE WORLD BROKEN APART~

Paper
It tears easily.
Rocks on the other hand don't tear
They shatter.
We as people do both.
We tear ourselves apart on the inside.
Some of us on the outside.
We shatter like glass the same.
What claws at us though?

The possible claws that tear us apart are vast.
But in this context, we're talking about the world as a whole,
That means everyone in attendance.
You might've noticed the consistent use of the phrase "we".
This is because this entire book revolves around "us".
The world and the earth are the same and different all the same.
We reside on them yet we make up the world,
The world is the environment we make it.
The earth is the land we live in.
You don't hear people saying it's a cold earth out there.
They say it's a cold world.
The world is hard.
I've hinted various times at the stature of the earth
But when I refer to us I'm referring to the people who make or break the atmosphere we live in.
The thing about tears that is interesting is that Tears can be mended.
If we look at fabric, it is quickly sewed.
If we look at paper, it can be taped.
If we look at muscle...well it can be mended.
When we look at bonds, it depends on what it was constructed upon.
This is another segment on relationships.
What are they constructed upon that they tear so easily?
Not even amongst friends but amongst people.

We hate each other easily but take years to try and love someone.
We fool ourselves by thinking everyone is an enemy and we tether a bond that never existed in our hearts.
We are torn by our own premonition.
We could connect with people if only we were willing to open up.
We have standards that are good but you never know who will inherit them.
People will surprise you with how much they watch.
The eyes are the window to the soul but they are the assessors of truth.
You can find out a lot about a person based on how they treat other people outside of you.
The same is true about groups,
This is where we are broken apart
We split ourselves into castes of an unnecessary nature.
We constantly try to change what is acceptable
Because we can't handle the truth
Because we're a childish race.
We whine like babies when things don't go our way.
When we're told no we throw a tantrum.
And when we want change we can't do anything but throw an angry fit.
If I am to say the truth,
The government is weak, altering laws to please the eye of abominable people.
We are not keeping the peace by letting evil slide through the doors.
We're just stirring up strife.

What happened to right and wrong
Acceptable and unacceptable
If you're getting riled up or offended right now I'm
talking to you.
Sometimes we have to hear the truth or we'll just
live a life of lies
Spread because the human accepted an inhumane
solution to evil.
Accepting it.
If you want me to be direct
There is a problem with homosexuality
There is an issue with transgender transitions
There is an issue with racial abuse
There is an issue with polytheism
There is an issue with evil.
There is an issue with murder
There is an issue with recreational drugs
There is an issue with drunkenness
There is an issue with excessive partying
There is an issue with thieving
There is an issue with sex outside of marriage
There is an issue with adultery
There is an issue with a plethora of other things we
choose to embark upon.
We are not born with these indications
No kid is born as such
They are either nurtured or fooled by the darkness
To move in such a manner.
Religion is a touchy topic but when science is
proving the evidence of religion, I'm confused.
Freedom of speech has faded because the truth is
too heavy for people to understand.

Have we not noticed the turmoil our world is
spiraling in?
Have we not noticed the unrest and the rise of
darkness amongst all nations?
We are broken.
Yet we try to fix it by destroying ourselves further.
We're destroying our nation's trying to please the
darkness.
People, we are losing our spark and we are dying
because of it.
We're encouraging the dark when the light rules
against it.
We are broken
As a bulb fixing to explode.
This earth,
This world
Is breaking apart.
Day by day
We are turning over to the wrong side.
People who fight for the light are ostracized
Because we fight for what is right.
Cancel culture is just a way for the dark to put
chains over those who care about keeping the
correct standard.
This world needs work
But after reading this section you've probably
already closed the book.
Like I said
We are a childish race, struggling to feed itself,
Trying to find ways to figure out how best to support
the majority a.k.a the dark.
We neglect the truth because we can't prove

It when the proof right in front of us.
We fight those who look different because they are born that way
Yet we defend those who openly commit abominations to the true law by which we should live.
The bible.
It tells us what's right and what's wrong
How to live and how to act
But since we cannot see the one who constructed it all
We don't follow those instructions because what?
Is man more influential than God?
We'll see in the end, won't we?
We are broken,
Stripping ourselves of the light we *could* posses
You can agree or disagree but as I said we'll see.
Our relationships are too focused on the dark,
This is why we are stumbling so much.
There is no peace in this world
And there is no unity.
There is no freedom in this world.
We are bound by the dark,
Take heed to what I said earlier and maybe if you pay attention you'll find the light.
The choice is yours.
We can't live like this forever,
We can't remain broken forever.
I'm talking to you,
The reader
There's got to be a change.
Choose the light, refuse the darkness.

This is the world we live in
And it's imploding.
We live in a broken world and a change has to
come.
I don't mean ridicule people, lend a hand and offer
them a choice
Freedom into the light
Or bondage in the darkness.
Hatred can't spread any longer
If you know something is wrong
Stand against it
Don't stand for it out of fear of being canceled
We all have a good idea of what's right and wrong
The choice is ours but we could at least try
Before all of the light of this world is diminished and
there is no chance for release.
No man is better than the next but we must know
when to call out the darkness and stand against it
lest we die.
This also means you yourself needs to take heed
and free yourself from the darkness.
Wield the catalyst for the light (the bible) and learn
the truth as to what is going on in this accursed
world.

~IT'S TIME TO START~
May you please give me the start?
That's the beginning
And I'll figure out the ending
It's much like life which is fleeting
I always asked for the beginning and
Tried hard to get the ending

But what does the middle mean?
Do all the trials
People,
Places,
Ideas,
Dreams,
Lifestyles,
Mean nothing?
I've been through the fire and ever since
I refused to go back until it's quenched.
My heart tells me I'm good enough
But my head says you're not cut
for that kind of stuff
I know it's a bluff
But I find it tough
To search in the middle
To recognize the ending.
In the middle I made friends
I lost friends.
In the middle I had dreams
And I chased dreams.
In the middle I had Doubts
I fought doubt.
In the middle I got bored
I felt excited.
In the middle, my heart broke
And it was fixed.
In the middle I found purpose
I chased purpose.
But everything in the middle is so hard to surface
Because those events were like a furnace
Hot, Uncomfortable, and burning

They should be shared
But if you give me the start
I'll figure out the ending.
As long as we continue blending.
So far I have given you the start
Love
Kindness
Extending a hand
Finding yourself
Stepping away from the darkness
Watching what you choose to digest
And It'd take a minute to list the rest
But this is but the start
Every action needs an initiator
And the world needs a catalyst for change.
Who amongst man is willing to embrace the openly
given access to the light?
The gunshot to start the race has already been
fired.
Now, it's up to us to either move away from the
block and flee the darkness
Or stay where we are and get engulfed by it.
A racer would know that in a track meet
They'd lose if they didn't move.
A lot of us are afraid of tripping or of falling over a
hurdle before we ever even begin.
This means that when the gun sounds
We hold back and lose sight of our goal of reaching
the finish line first.
In this race, it's a battle between ourselves,
But looking from left to right,
On the left, there is our best self.

On the right is our worst self,
And in the middle is us.
Who are you trying to exceed but more or less?
What are we going to do?
When the race begins all of you run
The worst you will stumble early and give up while
as your best you goes with their strides confident
even after a stumble, quickly getting up after each
mistake.
You could be right beside the best you, fighting to
surpass them,
Or you could stop early, in the middle, anywhere
and give up.
This race goes on forever
And if we're striving toward the light
Where love,
Passion,
Hope,
Compassion,
Etc resides,
The choice should be an easy one to decide
Where you'll ride.
Trials come with time.
The dark will graze your back and call to you
From behind.
But let the light be a sign
That there is still good in the world.
But there need to be runners carrying torches
For people to see and believe
That there's a possibility
Worthy of the title of succeeding.
A chance.

The chance for a brighter world.
This is important
You cannot do it all alone
We and I mean we as people need to join together
and stand for the truth,
For the light.
Our world is already dying
What do we have to lose?
Nothing but the increasing weight on our shoulders
generated by the dark.
It's about time to start doing something beyond
ourselves.
Once we find ourselves we'll realize that we aren't
On this earth to satisfy ourselves.
It's about time we start.
Take your feet off the block and run.
It's live or die,
Freedom or bondage.
We all need help,
We all need change and steering
In the right direction.
Move forward and away from the dark
No longer back and deeper into it.
This is the world we live in.
So we can be conscious as to what we're running
towards.
There's no excuse.
We know good from bad
Right from wrong
The choice is always ours.
Choose wisely.
The time for change is now.

3.

2.

1.

START!!!!

We can change the world,

Our new goal should be to leave the world a little better than whence we came.

But we once again have to start.

Runners take years to achieve their greatness;

The same applies to us.

We have to hone in on who we are and begin to execute.

This is a lifelong pursuit,

The light. So pursue it with everything you've got.

This is your race, this is OUR race, so run.

~THE WORLD~

So THIS is the world we live in.

The home, place, and den

Where we all live side by side together as kin.

At least that was how it was back then,

Or was it really?

I don't know what to tell you

But this world,

The world we live in today

 is far from unified.

Kinship does not exist in our realm

And we've long since given hatred the helm.

And it's driving us to hell

We've allowed evil to ring the bell

Of this world.

THIS world is struggling to survive, beaten by pride

Yet it can't fight for itself.

I'm sure you know this
But you're probably wondering why I'm immediately
bashing this world.
 I would be wrong to say that there is no good here
But I am saying that positive improvement is where
we need to be steered.
It only happens by our desire
The start of the wire.
Then we go on to relationships
The flavor of the chip before and after the dip.
We have to check our ambition.
It's the key in the ignition.
Our argument would be a lovely topic.
It's the number one thing that's continually toxic.
What about our attention,
Seems like we're all caught up in superstition.
We live in a world of misfits where everyone wants
a taste of acceptance but would rather change who
they are to be distanced.
What is the extent of our fame?
What is the extent of our fortune?
What is the extent of our happiness?
Our sadness?
Our joy?
Our peace?
What is the extent of our short, short lives?
What is the extent of the condition of our world?
Is this not our world?
Where we live,
Breathe,
Walk,

Talk,
Laugh,
Cry,
Dance,
Shout,
Pout,
But we are in a drought, my friend.
Without a reasonable doubt, we are losing our
connection with each other.
Social media,
I don't know, you tell me, is it really *social?*
Or is it just *media?*
What are we feeding ourselves that makes us so
divided?
This world's direction is fairly one-sided.
At least if we don't change.
We both know what this is, this is a call to action
And I'm relying on you and your reaction.
It's not for me but for THIS world.
For our world, our home until we die.
Will you join me for this ride in understanding what
we can do to make sure it is not our hand that tears
us apart.
Until we depart it's about time we start.
Our lives are each their own unique piece of art.
It doesn't matter if you're smart,
You could be a Bart.
It doesn't matter, be whoever you are as we go
through our world,
                    THIS WORLD, together.

www.ingramcontent.com/pod-product-compliance
Lightning Source LLC
Chambersburg PA
CBHW021411210526
45463CB00001B/315